Psychosomatic Disorders

THE STATE OF
MENTAL ILLNESS
AND ITS THERAPY

THE STATE OF MENTAL ILLNESS AND ITS THERAPY

Psychosomatic Disorders

Autumn Libal

Mason Crest

Mason Crest
450 Parkway Drive, Suite D
Broomall, PA 19008
www.masoncrest.com

Printed in the Hashemite Kingdom of Jordan.

First printing
9 8 7 6 5 4 3 2 1

Series ISBN: 978-1-4222-2819-7
ISBN: 978-1-4222-2834-0
ebook ISBN: 978-1-4222-8995-2

The Library of Congress has cataloged the
        hardcopy format(s) as follows:

        Library of Congress Cataloging-in-Publication Data

Libal, Autumn.
  [Drug therapy and psychosomatic disorders]
  Psychosomatic disorders / Autumn Libal.
      pages cm. – (The state of mental illness and its therapy)
  Originally published: Drug therapy and psychosomatic disorders / by Autumn Libal. 2004.
  Audience: 12.
  Audience: Grade 7 to 8.
  Includes index.
  ISBN 978-1-4222-2834-0 (hardcover) – ISBN 978-1-4222-2819-7 (series) – ISBN 978-1-4222-8995-2 (ebook)
  1. Medicine, Psychosomatic–Juvenile literature. 2. Medicine, Psychosomatic–Chemotherapy–Juvenile literature. 3. Medicine, Psychosomatic–Alternative treatment–Juvenile literature. I. Title.
  RC49.L465 2014
  616.08–dc23
                        2013008233

Produced by Vestal Creative Services.

www.vestalcreative.com

Picture credits:
Artville: pp. 30, 32, 41, 43, 56, 60, 66, 68, 71, 73, 76, 91. Buschmen | Dreamstime.com p. 113. Chin Han Low | Dreamstime.com: p. 31. Chris Niemann | Dreamstime.com: p. 101. Comstock: pp. 86, 94, 101, 102. Corbis: pp. 22, 89, 114, 115, 117, 120. Corel: pp. 10, 12, 44. Eduardsv | Dreamstime.com: p. 29. Gary Arbach | Dreamstime.com: p. 94. Lisa F. Young | Dreamstime.com: p. 82. Marsia16 | Dreamstime.com: p. 14. Monkey Business Images | Dreamstime.com: p. 116. National Library of Medicine: p. 112. PhotoAlto: pp: 19, 20, 38, 72, 92, 108. PhotoDisc: pp. 17, 26, 47, 52, 55, 74, 77, 78, 104, 106, 119. Rubberball: pp. 64, 98. Serialcoder | Dreamstime.com: p. 63. Sigurdur William Brynjarsson | Dreamstime.com: p. 86. Stockbyte: p. 32. Teprzem | Dreamstime.com: p. 110. The individuals in these images are models, and the images are for illustrative purposes only. To the best knowledge of the publisher, all other images are in the public domain. If any image has been inadvertantly uncredited or miscredited, please notify Vestal Creative Services, Vestal, New York 13850, so that rectification can be made for future printings.

CONTENTS

Introduction
by Mary Ann McDonnell

Teenagers have reason to be interested in psychiatric disorders and their treatment. Friends, family members, and even teens themselves may experience one of these disorders. Using scenarios adolescents will understand, this series explains various psychiatric disorders and the drugs that treat them.

Diagnosis and treatment of psychiatric disorders in children between six and eighteen years old are well studied and documented in the scientific journals. A paper appearing in the *Journal of the American Academy of Child and Adolescent Psychiatry* in 2010 estimated that 49.5 percent of all adolescents aged 13 to 18 were affected by at least one psychiatric disorder. Various other studies have reported similar findings. Needless to say, many children and adolescents are suffering from psychiatric disorders and are in need of treatment.

Many children have more than one psychiatric disorder, which complicates their diagnoses and treatment plans. Psychiatric disorders often occur together. For instance, a person with a sleep disorder may also be depressed; a teenager with attention-deficit/hyperactivity disorder (ADHD) may also have a substance-use disorder. In psychiatry, we call this comorbidity. Much research addressing this issue has led to improved diagnosis and treatment.

The most common child and adolescent psychiatric disorders are anxiety disorders, depressive disorders, and ADHD. Sleep disorders, sexual disorders, eating disorders, substance-abuse disorders, and psychotic disorders are also quite common. This series has volumes that address each of these disorders.

Major depressive disorders have been the most commonly diagnosed mood disorders for children and adolescents. Researchers don't agree as to how common mania and bipolar disorder are in children. Some experts believe that manic episodes in children and adolescents are underdiagnosed. Many times, a mood disturbance may occur with another psychiatric disorder. For instance, children with ADHD may also be depressed. ADHD is just one psychiatric disorder that is a major health concern for children, adolescents, and adults. Studies of ADHD have reported prevalence rates among children that range from two to 12 percent.

Failure to understand or seek treatment for psychiatric disorders puts children and young adults at risk of developing substance-use disorders. For example, recent research indicates that those with ADHD who were treated with medication were 85 percent less likely to develop a substance-use disorder. Results like these emphasize the importance of timely diagnosis and treatment.

Early diagnosis and treatment may prevent these children from developing further psychological problems. Books like those in this series provide important information, a vital first step toward increased awareness of psychological disorders; knowledge and understanding can shed light on even the most difficult subject. These books should never, however, be viewed as a substitute for professional consultation. Psychiatric testing and an evaluation by a licensed professional is recommended to determine the needs of the child or adolescent and to establish an appropriate treatment plan.

Foreword

by Donald Esherick

We live in a society filled with technology—from computers surfing the Internet to automobiles operating on gas and batteries. In the midst of this advanced society, diseases, illnesses, and medical conditions are treated and often cured with the administration of drugs, many of which were unknown thirty years ago. In the United States, we are fortunate to have an agency, the Food and Drug Administration (FDA), which monitors the development of new drugs and then determines whether the new drugs are safe and effective for use in human beings.

When a new drug is developed, a pharmaceutical company usually intends that drug to treat a single disease or family of diseases. The FDA reviews the company's research to determine if the drug is safe for use in the population at large and if it effectively treats the targeted illnesses. When the FDA finds that the drug is safe and effective, it approves the drug for treating that specific disease or condition. This is called the labeled indication.

During the routine use of the drug, the pharmaceutical company and physicians often observe that a drug treats other medical conditions besides what is indicated in the labeling. While the labeling will not include the treatment of the particular condition, a physician can still prescribe the drug to a patient with this disease. This is known as an unlabeled or off-label indication. This series contains information about both the labeled and off-label indications of psychiatric drugs.

I have reviewed the books in this series from the perspective of the pharmaceutical industry and the FDA, specifically focusing on the labeled indications, uses, and known side effects of these drugs. Further information can be found on the FDA's website (www.FDA.gov).

Those who serve their nation in the armed forces face many dangers, both physical and emotional.

Chapter One

What Are Psychosomatic Disorders?

Kevin always knew that even peacekeeping missions were dangerous, but he also knew that the goal of peace was worth the personal risks. He firmly believed that for peace to exist in the world every person had to make a commitment and be willing to accept sacrifices for the greater good. In some ways, Kevin saw the loss of his right leg as proof of his dedication to making the world a better place. He believed so firmly in the mission of peacekeeping that he would give his life for the cause, and every day his missing limb reminded him that in April of 1999 he nearly did just that.

For three months his unit had been moving across the outskirts of the village with painstaking slowness, clearing the area of land mines, mortar shells, and unexploded grenades. Combat soldiers no longer roamed the streets, but for the children of this village these fields were still a war zone. Many of the village's youth bore the scars from childhood games played in the aftermath of battle.

On that spring day in war-torn Kosovo, Kevin stepped on a land mine. Accidents were a part of the job, a danger for which everyone trained. But nothing could have prepared Kevin for how fast his life changed that day. The momentum of the blast was so great that Kevin felt the sand, stone, and heated shards of metal ripping into his body before the sound of the explosion even hit his ears. He slipped in and out of a dim consciousness as he was rushed into the military

Combat requires great bravery—before, during, and after the actual battle.

hospital where doctors fought to save him. After surgery, infection set in, and he spent the next two weeks in a feverish delirium. Days went by as he lay unconscious, oblivious to everything around him. But one day, the pain of his right leg finally screamed through the cloud of illness, forcing Kevin's eyes open. It was as if the pain were a beacon sent to cut through the blackness of oblivion, pierce the veil of death, and pull him back into the living world again.

When Kevin opened his eyes to this new, pain-racked world, a sudden calm washed over him. The physical suffering brought his life into sudden focus, forcing him to think about his body so that he could assess the damage. He tried sitting up to look around, but the pain was too great. He could not move to see his body, so staring at the bare fluorescent bulb above him, he began a mental evaluation of his condition. Beginning with the top of his head, he concentrated on each part of his body, the way it felt and moved, trying to determine the extent of his injuries. He lifted his eyebrows and blinked his eyes; they were a bit sensitive to the harsh lights, but other than that they felt fine. He licked his lips and tried opening his mouth. His lips felt cracked and parched, like sandpaper worn thin with use. His jaw was stiff and sore, and he felt scabs and stitches stretching as his facial muscles strained. He tried to turn his head, but a thick neck brace prevented any movement. He took a deep breath and felt his chest rise and fall, lungs still scorched by sand and burning fumes. Working down his body, he wiggled each finger, tilted his hips, tortuously flexed his screaming knees, and wiggled each toe. Despite his tremendous discomfort, a deep sigh of relief escaped his body. The pain was incredible but at least everything was intact, he thought. Each limb, joint, finger, and toe accounted for. Truly a miracle, he thought, that all the parts of him had survived, especially his right leg, which shrieked the loudest with pain.

After waking up, Kevin went on for two more days believing he still had both legs. A morphine cloud dulled his senses to the movement and talk around him. He had no reason to doubt the existence of his right leg, because he could feel it lying there next to his left one. The leg was the focus of the greatest pain he'd ever experi-

Placebos are pills made from some harmless substance that lacks any actual medicinal value. The mind is so powerful, though, that a person may get better simply because he believes he is taking a potent medicine.

enced, but at least he could wiggle his toes and flex his knee. He had a maddening itch that ran from his ankle to his thigh, and he assumed it must be the itch of a healing wound.

On Kevin's third day awake he found out the shocking truth. A nurse had come around to bathe him and change his bandages. He smiled at her as she began washing his neck and arms. He mustered the strength to lift his head—and then she pulled the sheet back from his body. Kevin stared, as shocked as if the land mine had blown up in his face all over again. Where his right leg was supposed to be—where he felt pain, itching, movement, and even the touch of the scratchy hospital sheets against his skin—was nothing but a bandaged stump below his thigh and an empty space where his leg should have been.

Our minds can do powerful things. For example, in medical research doctors gave sick patients something ordinary, like a sugar pill, but told the patients that they were receiving powerful medication. Some of the patients who were given the sugar pill got better. Scientists determined that the patients were cured simply because they believed that the medicine would cure them. What cured the patients was not the pill but the power of their own minds. This is a psychosomatic reaction called the placebo effect.

The placebo effect, however, can also work in the opposite direction. When researchers gave patients sugar pills, but told the patients that they were being given medications that could produce negative side effects, some of the patients developed the side effects regardless of the fact that they were taking a harmless sugar pill. The side effects that the patients experienced resulted from the same type of psychosomatic reactions that patients with somatoform disorders experience.

Three years later, back in his home in St. Catherine's, Ontario, Kevin sometimes still had trouble believing his leg was truly gone. He often had strange sensations he could not explain. Some were unpleasant, like the constant itching where he no longer had a place to itch. Others were nice surprises, like when he could feel his cat brushing against where his leg should be. The worst, however, was the pain. All the other inexplicable feelings would come and go, but the pain in his leg never left his body or his mind. Sometimes in the dark quiet of his bedroom he had nightmares in which he relived stepping on the land mine. Only in his nightmares, everything happened in slow motion, and he could see his leg tearing away from his body. He would reach forward, grabbing for his leg; then the excruciating pain would wake him up.

He would lie, panting in the darkness, trying to will away the pain. He constantly asked himself how something that didn't even exist could hurt so badly. Worst of all, nothing seemed to help. Additional surgeries and painkillers, including morphine, seemed helpless against this evil phantom that tortured him night and day.

Discussion

Psychosomatic disorders are some of the most intriguing and mysterious illnesses in all of medicine. The term "psycho" means something relating to the mind. The term "somatic" means something relating to the physical or biological body. A psychosomatic disorder consists of bodily symptoms—like pain, nausea, or dizziness—that appear to be created by the mind. The term "psychosomatic," although accurately describing the nature of these illnesses, is generally used in common speech. The medical term that is most often used for such illnesses is "somatoform disorders." The defining feature of somatoform illnesses is that the patient suffers from a physical illness for which there is no apparent physical or biological cause.

When patients have physical symptoms that cannot be diagnosed according to current definitions of disease, doctors tend to classify these symptoms as psychological. This happens largely because Western medicine practices what is known as "evidence-based medicine." In evidence-based medicine, doctors rely on

Western: Relating to the culture of Europe and America.

objective: Based on evidence observable to someone other than the person affected.

subjective: The sense of perspective on an experience from the affected person's point of view.

objective proof of illness rather than on patients' subjective reports of personal experience. The objective proof of disease that the doctor looks for is biological or physical evidence of illness, such as a virus in the bloodstream or a tumor in an organ. If biological evidence is not found, the symptoms are assumed to be psychological, meaning that the cause of the physical symptoms is in the mind, not the body. Many aspects of the mind–body relationship remain a mystery to modern medicine. We still do not fully understand the mind's role in the experience of illness and pain.

A dramatic example of the mind's power over the physical body can be seen in Kevin's story. Kevin is suffering from a somatoform pain disorder in which he feels pain in his leg even after that leg has been amputated. At first, Kevin's story may seem unbelievable. How can someone have sensations like touch and pain in a part of the body that doesn't even exist? As difficult as it might be to believe, Kevin is actually experiencing something that is quite common

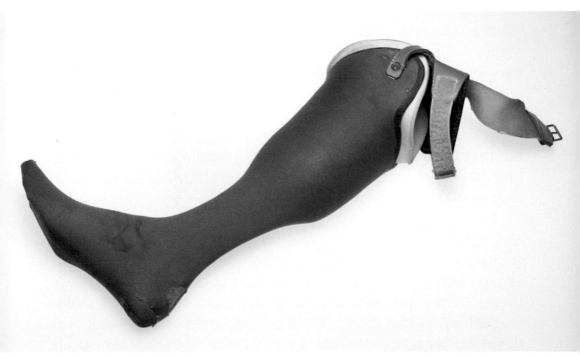

A person with a prosthetic leg may still "feel" his real leg.

among people who have had amputations. The pain Kevin feels is known as phantom-limb pain, a mysterious disorder that is especially widespread among people who lost limbs in traumatic events, such as those associated with war.

Phantom-limb pain and other similar disorders provide a fascinating look into the complicated interactions of the body and the mind. Such disorders also show us that despite incredible advances in modern medicine, many things about psychosomatic disorders are still unsolved puzzles. In the above case, Kevin feels pain in his leg, but no physical leg exists to create that pain. What is this pain and where does it come from? Doctors have many theories about this type of pain, but the only thing that we can say for sure is that Kevin's pain is caused by some complicated interaction between his body and his brain that we do not fully understand.

Despite the fact that physical symptoms are often psychosomatic in nature, labeling physical symptoms as psychological can be misleading for two reasons. The first is that medical knowledge is changing all the time. Researchers are constantly discovering previously unknown causes and treatments for diseases, rethinking faulty medical assumptions of the past. Sometimes people's disorders are misdiagnosed as psychological not because the symptoms are caused by psychological factors but because modern medicine does not have the tools to identify the physical cause of the illness. Many people also tend to interpret "psychological" as "imagined"— but that is not always the case. For all these reasons, doctors must take great care when diagnosing a patient's physical symptoms as psychosomatic or somatoform disorders.

To understand the psychosomatic aspect of pain and illness more clearly, try to think of times when the pain or discomfort you felt changed because of your mental state. For example, have you ever experienced an injury that did not hurt until you realized it was there? Maybe you were chopping vegetables and did not realize that you sliced your thumb. The moment, however, that you looked down and recognized the blood as your own, your thumb began to throb. Have you ever injured yourself in the middle of a highly com-

If we injure a finger without realizing we have done so, we may be unaware of the pain—until we notice what we have done.

petitive sports game but only realized you were injured once you got off the field, or even the next day? Perhaps everyone in your family had the flu, but you needed to stay well for a big test in school. The minute you finished the test, however, you suddenly came down with a flu that was worse than anyone else had experienced. In common examples like these, the physical experience of pain and illness was not solely dependent on sensory stimulation. There was also a mental, **cognitive** aspect to the experience. Feeling the pain of cutting your thumb depended on mentally recognizing that an injury had occurred. While your mind was focused on the fast-paced competition of the game, you did not realize you sustained an injury. When you needed to be well for a test, your body fought off the illness until the test was completed.

cognitive: Relating to mental awareness or reasoning.

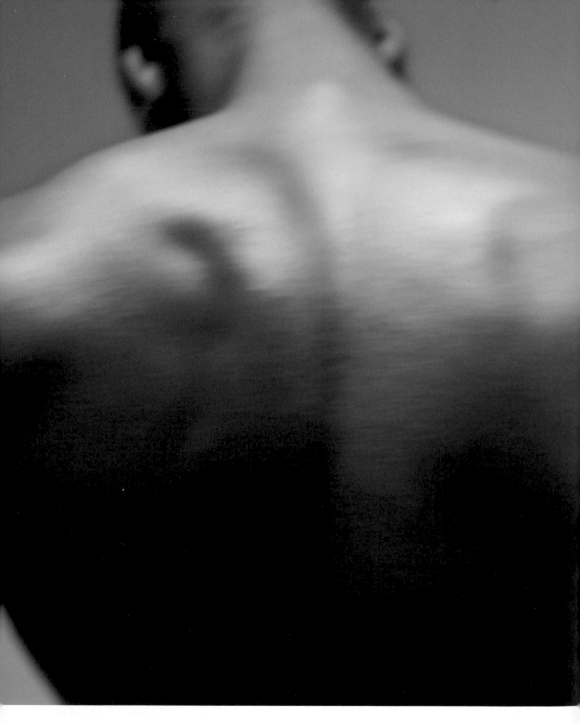

North Americans react to back pain differently from people in other cultures.

All of the above are examples of pain or illness that have physical causes. These examples of pain and illness are therefore not considered psychosomatic. However, through these examples we see that even physically based pain and illness involve the mind. In both physical and psychosomatic disorders, the fact that your mental state plays a role in how you experience your pain or illness does not necessarily mean that the pain or illness is any less real or severe. It simply means that the disorder is not caused just by your body.

Not only do internal processes such as thoughts and emotions affect the psychosomatic nature of illness and pain, but external factors influence our psychosomatic reactions as well. Cultural attitudes toward certain types of pain and illnesses can affect how individuals experience the pain or illness.

For example, some studies have shown that North American patients with back injuries are less likely to recover and may even feel the pain more acutely than patients of other cultures. These studies suggest that one of the reasons North Americans react to back injuries differently is that North American culture sees chronic back pain as a disability and even offers disability insurance for such conditions. These studies are not saying that the patients are faking or intentionally extending their illnesses. Instead, the studies suggest that the brain's awareness of these cultural conditions triggers the person's body to behave differently in different cultural atmospheres. A person living in North America, where disability insurance covers the cost of a work-related back injury, may feel so much pain from a back injury that she is unable to return to work for six months. However, another person, who has the same type of injury but lives in a country that does not have disability insurance, heals and is able to return to work in one month.

Another common example of cultural differences in the experience of pain is that Western women tend to give birth in hospitals, report large amounts of pain, often request pain-reducing drugs, and require a significant recovery period. Women in some other cultures, however, give birth alone and without medication, report little pain, and may return to work the same day as giving birth.

The differences in how individuals experience their symptoms are the psychosomatic or somatoform aspects of their condition. There are a number of specific somatoform illnesses, and each has features doctors look for to diagnose the disorder.

Somatization Disorder

According to the *Diagnostic and Statistical Manual of Mental Disorders, fourth edition, text revision* (DSM-IV-TR), somatization disorder is a condition involving multiple physical complaints with no known physical cause. To be diagnosed with somatization disorder, these physical complaints must include some specific symptoms. First, the patient must have experienced pain in at least four different parts or

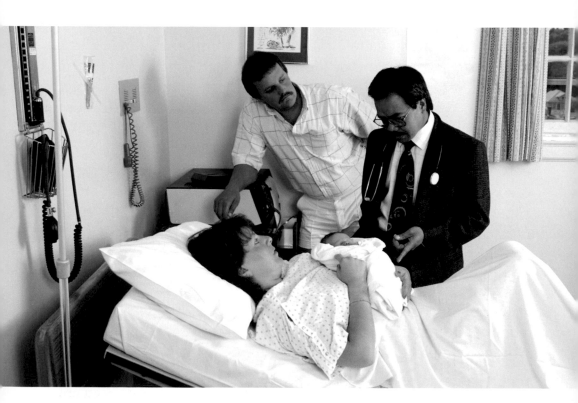

North American and European women perceive childbirth as more painful than women do in other areas of the world.

functions of her body. For example, she might feel pain in her back, joints, head, chest, or while urinating or menstruating. Unexplained pain, however, is not the only criteria for somatization disorder. In addition to the pain that she experiences, she must have at least two gastrointestinal symptoms, such as nausea or diarrhea. The patient must also have at least one non-pain symptom involving the reproductive system. An example for women could be irregular menstruation, and an example for men would be **erectile dysfunction**. The patient must also have at least one symptom that appears to be **neurological** in nature. Symptoms that suggest neurological dysfunction include dizziness, paralysis, loss of sensation, or seizures. The pain, gastrointestinal, reproductive, and neurological symptoms need not all be present at the same time, but a patient must have a medical history involving all these different symptoms in order to be diagnosed with somatization disorder.

erectile dysfunction: The inability to achieve an erect penis.

neurological: Related to the nervous system.

In addition to the different physical criteria for somatization disorder, there is also an age requirement for diagnosis. In order for a person to be diagnosed with somatization disorder, all the required symptoms must appear before the person is thirty years old, must last or recur for at least several years, and have a significant negative impact on the person's normal functioning. The major reason for an age requirement in diagnosis is that our bodies begin to deteriorate as we age. After age thirty, the simple effects of aging could cause many of the symptoms seen in somatization disorder—such as back pain, food intolerance, irregular menstruation, and erectile dysfunction—and a diagnosis of somatization disorder would be inappropriate.

A person with somatization disorder is not faking or intentionally creating her symptoms. Nevertheless, medical and laboratory examinations will fail to find any specific physical or biological cause for the symptoms. Some patients with somatization disorder will have ad-

manifestations: Forms or materializations of something's presence or existence.

motor functions: Movements.

factitious: Artificially produced or fake.

ditional general medical conditions. In cases of somatization disorder in which the patient does have a general medical condition (like a hormone imbalance, for example), the medical condition cannot fully explain all the symptoms the patient is experiencing.

Culture plays a large part in how patients experience somatization disorder. In African and South Asian countries, patients often report neurological symptoms such as feeling ants crawling under the skin or burning hands, whereas patients in the United States report neurological symptoms such as loss of balance and localized paralysis. Both groups of patients are suffering from psychosomatic neurological conditions, but different cultural influences cause them to have different physical **manifestations** of their illnesses.

Conversion Disorder

Conversion disorder is a somatoform disorder in which the major symptoms, such as dizziness, seizures, or numbness, appear to be neurological but are caused by psychological factors. A person with a conversion disorder experiences symptoms (beyond those of pain or sexual dysfunction) involving his sensory or **motor functions**, and these symptoms are triggered or exacerbated by emotional and stressful events. These symptoms are not intentional, **factitious**, caused by a general medical condition, or induced through the use or abuse of substances like medications, drugs, or alcohol. The symptoms must be distressing enough to significantly impact the patient's life and functioning.

There are four types of conversion disorders. The first is conversion disorder with motor symptom or deficit. In this type of

Somatoform disorders are different from two specific disorders known as factitious disorder and malingering. In factitious disorder, a person pretends to have an illness for personal gain. Perhaps the person wishes to avoid certain responsibilities, like employment, or wants to collect insurance money. The fake symptoms that a person creates in factitious disorder are very different from the psychologically based but completely real symptoms that a person with a somatoform disorder experiences. In malingering, a patient exaggerates a general medical condition or pretends to still be sick even after he has recovered in order to continue receiving the benefits, such as kind treatment, personal care, or monetary compensation, that he received while ill.

conversion disorder, the patient's symptoms are related to movement over which he would normally have voluntary control. For example, a person with a conversion disorder involving motor symptoms may not be able to move his limbs or may have an uncontrollable tic in his facial muscles. The second type of conversion disorder is conversion disorder with sensory symptom or deficit. In this type of conversion disorder, the patient experiences symptoms involving his senses of touch, taste, smell, hearing, or vision. Examples of sensory symptoms or deficits could include symptoms like hearing things that are not there, loss of taste, blurred vision, or numbness in parts of the body. The third type of conversion disorder is conversion disorder with seizures, in which a patient experiences nonepileptic seizures or other types of uncontrolled, convulsive movements. The final type of conversion disorder is

tic: An involuntary, repetitive movement or spasm.

seizures: Convulsions caused by sudden discharges of electrical activity in the brain.

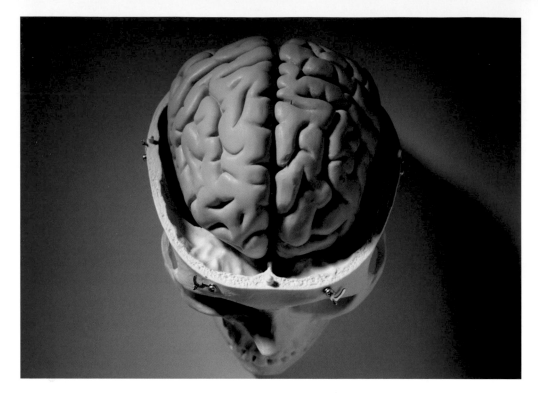

Doctors and scientists still struggle to understand the human brain. As a result, neurological disorders are often misdiagnosed as conversion disorders.

conversion disorder with mixed presentation, in which a patient experiences a combination of motor, sensory, seizure, and convulsive symptoms.

Conversion disorders usually occur between the ages of ten and thirty-five. After age thirty-five, the likelihood that one's neurological symptoms are caused by a physical medical condition instead of a psychological condition greatly increases. Some studies have shown that as many as one half of all people diagnosed with conversion disorders are later diagnosed with a general medical condition. The reason that misdiagnosis is so common in conversion disorder is that the individual's symptoms relate to the nervous system, a bodily system that still holds many mysteries for the medical field. In some cases, a doctor may at first be unable to find the physical cause for a person's neurological condition. The doctor may decide that the cause of the condition must be psychological and diagnose the patient with a conversion disorder. However, years later, as advances in technology and research bring new information and diagnostic tools to the medical field, the true physical cause of the individual's disorder may be found and treated.

Another reason that neurological disorders may be misdiagnosed as conversion disorders is that many neurological disorders, such as multiple sclerosis and Lyme disease, can have nonspecific, varying, and seemingly unrelated symptoms, especially in the early stages of the disease. Doctors and patients can become frustrated with the vague nature of neurological symptoms and overlook possible physical causes of the condition. This can happen not only when diagnosing conversion disorders but when diagnosing any apparent somatic disorder. A person with a conversion or other somatic disorder should have his diagnosis reviewed periodically in the event that new symptoms or recent advances in the medical field might provide further insight into his medical condition.

Pain Disorder

A person with pain disorder experiences pain that is severe enough to require medical attention and to have a significant negative impact on her normal functioning. Rather than being caused by an identifiable medical condition, the pain appears to be caused or exacerbated by psychological factors but is neither faked nor intentionally caused. There are two types of somatoform pain disorder.

The first type is pain disorder associated with psychological factors. An example of physical pain caused by a psychological factor can be seen in something known as "sympathetic labor pains." When a child is born, the child's mother experiences pain while in labor. Sometimes, however, the father also experiences sharp abdominal pain during the child's delivery. These pains, for which there is no physical cause, are thought to be caused by the father's psychological

acute onset: Developing quickly and without warning. Having a brief but severe course.

chronic: Lasting for a long time or occurring repeatedly.

prognosis: A prediction for the course and likelihood of recovering from a disease.

identification with and desire to participate in the birth process.

The second type of somatoform pain disorder is pain disorder associated with both psychological factors and a general medical condition. In the story at the beginning of the chapter, Kevin suffers from the specific medical condition of having an amputated limb. However, once his wounds are healed, the physical effects of the amputation cannot fully explain all of the pain he experiences, so his pain is diagnosed as a somatoform pain disorder associated with both psychological factors and a general medical condition.

A person experiencing acute onset psychosomatic pain will usually cease feeling pain once the immediate psychological stimulus ends. For example, the father experiencing psychosomatic abdominal pain during the mother's labor will cease feeling pain once the child is born. People who experience chronic psychosomatic pain, however, have a poorer prognosis for complete recovery. Furthermore, chronic pain associated with somatoform pain disorders does not respond well to painkillers and other drugs prescribed for pain management. Individuals with somatoform pain disorders often develop substance abuse disorders through the process of taking multiple kinds and increasing doses of drugs in an effort to control the pain. People with chronic pain disorders also appear to be at a higher risk for suicide.

Hypochondriasis

Hypochondriasis (also called hypochondria) is a psychological condition in which a person becomes fixated on a fear of contracting or

People experiencing somatoform pain disorders may abuse alcohol to help them cope with the pain they experience. This
"self-medication" is destructive and only adds to the person's
problems.

A person with hypochondriasis may be obsessed with thoughts of illness—or he may interpret minor symptoms as more dangerous than they really are.

the belief of having a serious disease or illness. Patients with hypochondriasis might have fewer physical symptoms than patients with other somatoform disorders, but the patient with hypochondriasis experiences greater mental and emotional distress by misinterpreting these symptoms as far more serious than they actually are. A small skin irregularity may convince her that she has skin cancer. After seeing a television news story about West Nile virus, she may be sure her slightly upset stomach means she has contracted the disease.

People often see a doctor about a symptom that turns out to be harmless. In fact, you may have experienced something like this yourself. Seeking a doctor's advice concerning a minor physical

A person with hypochondriasis is convinced that her symptoms are serious. She may go to many doctors seeking a medical practitioner who will confirm her fears.

When someone with hypochondriasis suffers from the common cold, he may be convinced he is dying of some dreadful disease!

The academic field of sociology studies a social position known as the "sick role." According to sociology, different cultural influences teach us how a person should act and be treated when she is sick. In North American culture, a person who is sick is expected to rest, refrain from work, and rely on others for her care. Individuals with factitious disorder and malingering may fake illness in order to gain access to the benefits of the sick role. Some doctors and sociologists believe that many somatoform disorders are also caused by the patients' unconscious desire to benefit from the care, attention, and treatment that the sick role provides.

symptom does not mean a person has a disorder like hypochondria. In most cases, a person is relieved and reassured by the doctor's advice and ceases to worry about the benign symptom. In contrast, a person with hypochondriasis cannot be reassured or convinced about the harmless nature or lack of existence of physical symptoms. However, contrary to popular belief, this preoccupation with sickness is not delusional. A patient with hypochondria may be fully aware that her fears are unwarranted, overzealous, or unreasonable. Nevertheless, she cannot release herself from her concerns. She may seek second, third, fourth, and even more opinions looking for a physician who will validate her illness.

benign: Harmless.

delusional: Holding incorrect beliefs despite all evidence to the contrary.

validate: To support or make official.

Being preoccupied with physical conditions and fears of illness is not enough to diagnose a patient as having hypochondria. In addition to the preoccupation with bodily concerns, the individual's fears must have a significant, negative impact on her life, affecting her social, familial, occupational, or other important areas of functioning. The condition must last for more than six months and not be caused by another disorder such as obsessive-compulsive disorder, panic disorder, anxiety disorder, or other psychological conditions. (To find out more about these psychological disorders, see the other titles in this series.)

anorexia nervosa: An eating disorder characterized by the inability to maintain a normal weight for height, age, and bone structure, along with an intense fear of gaining weight and a denial of the seriousness of the condition.

Body Dysmorphic Disorder

Individuals with body dysmorphic disorder have a severe and excessive preoccupation with a real or imagined bodily defect. To be considered a somatoform disorder, this excessive worry about a physical flaw must have a significant impact on the individual's ability to function normally and must not be better accounted for by another psychological disorder, such as anorexia nervosa.

A patient with body dysmorphic disorder begins to see slight physical irregularities or "flaws" as serious deformities. So much of his time becomes devoted to examining and worrying about his "defect" that it can become the dominant focus of his life. He may become suspicious of others, feeling they are also focused on the defect or discussing his defect when he is not around. Unlike hypochondria, in which a person's concerns do not reach delusional proportions, a person with body dysmorphic disorder may become delusional about the existence or seriousness of a body "defect."

Some of the most common physical attributes that individuals with body dysmorphic disorder focus on are scars, hair loss, and wrinkles, especially in the head and facial region. People with this disorder also often focus on the shape and size of facial features like the nose, eyes, eyebrows, mouth, and teeth. Preoccupation with the size and shape of breasts, hips, and genitals is common in women, while worry about the size and functioning of the penis is common in men. Individuals' concerns may also focus on more general complaints such as body size, weight, and muscularity.

Body dysmorphic disorder appears to be more common in cultures like that of North America, where the popular media is highly image oriented and extreme amounts of emphasis are placed on physical appearance. Body dysmorphic disorder is thought to be experienced among men as often as among women.

Undifferentiated Somatoform Disorder

In undifferentiated somatoform disorder, the patient suffers one or more somatic complaints but does not meet the diagnostic criteria for one of the specific somatoform disorders discussed previously. Like other somatoform disorders, the patient's symptoms cannot be explained by any physical or general medical condition and must be severe enough to significantly affect the patient's social, familial, occupational, or other functioning. The patient must not be faking or intentionally inducing the symptoms, and his condition must last for six months or more.

Somatoform Disorder Not Otherwise Specified

This classification of somatoform disorder is reserved for somatic illnesses that do not meet any of the above descriptions. An example is pseudocyesis, a psychosomatic condition in which a woman believes she is pregnant and experiences many of the symptoms of pregnancy. The woman may even experience an enlarging abdomen and labor pains at the expected time of birth, despite the fact

somatization: Convert-
ing mental or emo-
tional experiences into
physical sensations or
symptoms.

that she is not actually pregnant. The classification of somatoform disorder not otherwise specified is also given to psychosomatic symptoms that last for less than six months.

Depression and anxiety usually accompany somatoform disorders. It is not clear, however, if depression and anxiety are part of the cause of these disorders or if they are the result of living with these illnesses and the turmoil they bring. Depression and anxiety probably play some role in both the cause and the effects of these illnesses. In fact, they are so closely associated with somatization that some doctors now believe that making an independent illness category for somatization is senseless. Doctors of this mind-set tend to believe that if the mind is unwell, the body will perform poorly, and if the body is performing poorly, the mind becomes unwell. Part of the diagnosis for clinical depression (considered a mental disorder) is the presence of physical symptoms such as tiredness, aching joints, and loss of appetite—the very same types of physical symptoms associated with somatoform disorders. Just as depression can bring on physical symptoms, so can long-term physical symptoms like fatigue and pain bring on depression. When one feels sick, it is easy to begin feeling depressed and pessimistic.

Somatoform disorders not only resemble depression; they also resemble other psychiatric disorders. Anxiety disorder contains symptoms like those of somatoform and conversion disorders (racing heart, for example, and neurological symptoms in response to stress). Obsessive-compulsive disorder shares many of the same symptoms as hypochondriasis and body dysmorphic disorder. Many of the symptoms that appear in somatoform disorders also appear in personality disorders, dissociative disorders, and post-traumatic stress disorder.

If a person's pain or illness is created by his mind, does that mean that his pain or illness is not real? The answer is no. The more medicine learns about the interaction of the mind and body, the more our society recognizes that somatization is a normal and prevalent part of our everyday lives. Our bodies are constantly reacting to mental stimulation. When reliving the winning goal you made in the hockey game, your face might flush, heart race, and muscles tense. A child who is being bullied at school might feel sick every morning before leaving home. Seeing someone become ill may make you suddenly nauseated. A passionate kiss in the movies might make your own lips tingle. Understanding that the mind plays an important part in the way the physical body performs, including how a person experiences illness and pain, is essential to understanding what somatoform illnesses are and how they can be treated.

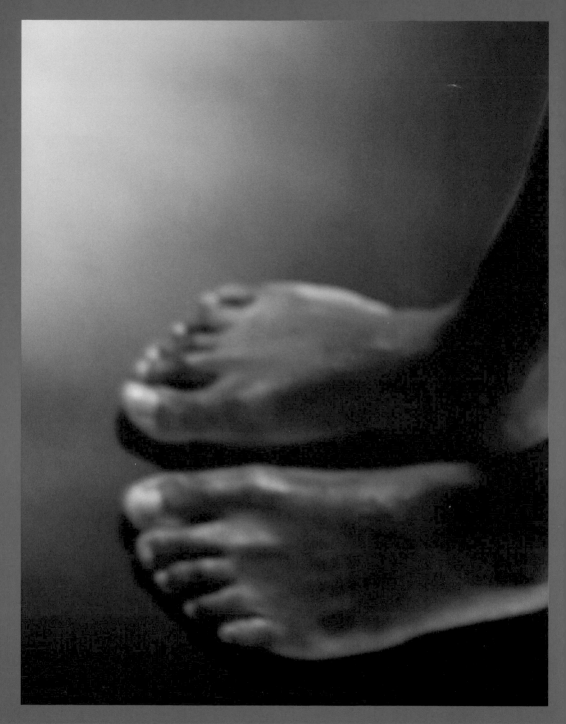

A person with a somatoform disorder may experience unexplained feelings of numbness in her feet or hands. She may feel as though her feet or other body parts are separated from her and no longer belong to her.

Chapter Two

History of Therapy and Drug Treatment

Jacquelyn's mysterious symptoms began when she was sixteen years old. She had just received her learner's permit and her father had taken her out for a drive. She was sitting at an intersection, waiting for the traffic to clear, when the bottom of her right foot went suddenly numb. Suddenly panicked, she tried explaining to her father that she could not feel the gas pedal beneath her foot. He told her to relax, that she was just nervous. But Jacquelyn's panic grew, and she refused to drive any further. They had to switch drivers while a line of impatient drivers honked their horns. Disappointed, her father drove them home.

The numbness in Jacquelyn's foot came and went for three months. Then it disappeared completely, departing as suddenly as it had come. But at the same time, she began having trouble swallowing and her vision grew blurry. The fear that had been building in her grew. For the past three months, Jacquelyn's parents thought she was just imagining things, but now they were alarmed as well. Finally, they took her to see a doctor.

After numerous tests, the doctor proclaimed there was nothing wrong with Jacquelyn—at least nothing he could identify. He asked many questions about her school, friends, and family life. Was she feeling under more pressure than usual? Did she sleep well at night? Did she notice any correlation between her emotions and her physical symptoms? Jacquelyn thought about these questions and thought that perhaps she was under more stress than usual. After all, she was learning to drive, had a lead role in the school play, was beginning to consider colleges, and volunteered at a soup kitchen on the weekends. Her doctor said that perhaps she was suffering from a conversion disorder, a psychological disorder in which her brain was translating mental and emotional stresses into physical neurological symptoms. He suggested that she see a therapist in addition to continuing her regular medical checkups.

Jacquelyn began seeing a therapist once a week. She enjoyed these sessions. They were a relaxing time when she found she could unwind and talk about anything that happened to be on her mind. Jacquelyn's therapist also taught her many stress-management techniques that she found helpful for organizing her time and dealing with daily challenges. Nevertheless, her neurological symptoms seemed unchanged. They waxed and waned. Sometimes Jacquelyn thought she was getting better only to have a new and mysterious symptom unexpectedly appear. Her therapist seemed perplexed by these shifting symptoms as well. Two years into therapy, depression began pulling Jacquelyn down. She was working so hard and had learned many skills, but her physical symptoms still had not subsided. Her therapist prescribed Prozac for the depression.

Three years after her treatment began, Jacquelyn's therapist thought that perhaps it was time to revisit her original diagnosis.

Stress-management techniques allow the individual to find a place of mental peace even during moments of external tension.

According to the theory that somatoform disorders are the result of unresolved, repressed emotional trauma, a patient who suffered physical abuse as a child might develop a somatoform disorder in the following way. Perhaps the patient is unable to remember the abuse because the memories are so emotionally overwhelming that her mind has blocked them from view. The emotional turmoil and conflict that remains buried and unresolved begins to manifest itself as physical symptoms such as gastrointestinal difficulties and fatigue. Whenever she experiences stressful or emotionally painful events, especially situations that could trigger memories of the abuse, her arms and legs go numb, she begins to feel dizzy, and is overcome by a sudden sense of weakness. In a situation like this one, a doctor may theorize that the woman's brain, when threatened with uncomfortable situations and memories, triggers her body to respond in physical ways. This sudden onset of physical symptoms draws the woman's attention away from the emotionally threatening situation, thus protecting her against remembering and reliving her past sufferings.

Together with Jacquelyn's regular doctor, they reviewed Jacquelyn's entire medical history, her progress in therapeutic treatment, and how her symptoms had changed over time. Jacquelyn's doctor began a new round of diagnostic tests. At the end of this series of tests, they found that Jacquelyn had not been suffering from a somatoform conversion disorder but from an illness known as multiple sclerosis. This disorder of the central nervous system had evaded their detection for three years. Jacquelyn, however, was not upset about the time she had spent in therapy, for she had learned many skills there that would aid her in accepting and dealing with the chronic disease.

When a person is taking medication and yet continues to experience symptoms of pain and discomfort, it may be time to consider a new diagnosis.

Discussion

Over time and in different cultures there have been many explanations for somatoform illnesses. For instance, somatic symptoms used to be called hysteria. In Greek civilization, hysteria was thought to occur only in women; the word comes from the Greek word hys-

The Egyptians believed that a woman's maladies were often caused by her uterus moving around her body.

tera, which means "uterus." The Greeks thought that the woman's uterus became dislodged from its normal location and would travel around the woman's body, causing pain or illness wherever it went. Interestingly, four thousand years ago the Egyptians also explained hysteria in the same way; they also believed that the uterus traveled about the body, causing illness and pain. This explanation for hysteria shows that even long ago people sought physical explanations for physical symptoms.

This has not always been the case. Before science discovered microorganisms like bacteria and began understanding the internal systems of the body, illnesses were believed to be punishments for sins and transgressions— not the result of airborne viruses, malignant growths, or eating bad meat. In the present-day Western world, illness is seen as a matter for scientists and doctors, but in the Middle Ages, illness was a topic for philosophers and theologians, as much a matter of the spirit and mind as of the body. In those times, it was easy for people to believe that physical symptoms could be caused by a nonphysical influence.

theologians: Scholars of religion, God, and spiritual questions.

Enlightenment: A philosophical movement in the eighteenth century that emphasized rationalism and science and deemphasized religion, spirituality, and mysticism.

modernism: Conforming to modern ideas and principles, examining traditional beliefs according to current knowledge and philosophy.

demystify: To remove all mystery, give concrete explanation.

With the Enlightenment era and modernism, however, science sought to demystify nature and the world. People began to believe that there was a rational, scientifically based reason for everything, that every mystery could be solved through scientific investigation and every pain and illness could be understood and treated through

biomedicine. Throughout the nineteenth and twentieth centuries, Western biomedicine has constructed bodily definitions of pain and illness as the body's reaction to physical stimuli, making it difficult for doctors and patients to believe that their physical symptoms could be caused by legitimate emotional and mental concerns. If doctors disregard patients' psychosomatic symptoms, somatoform disorders become almost impossible to respect and treat adequately.

biomedicine: An approach to medicine that applies the "objective" principles of natural science to diagnosing, understanding, and treating disease. This approach to medicine focuses on the physical and observable body rather than the subjective mind.

Not all Western scientists have believed that physical symptoms must have physical causes. In 1859, a scientist named Paul Briquet explained somatic symptoms as the result of a person's mind converting emotional turmoil into physical ailments. For much of the latter half of the twentieth century, in fact, somatization disorder was known as Briquet's syndrome. In the early twentieth century, Sigmund Freud (the father of psychoanalysis) had his own explanation for hysteria (or what we now refer to as somatoform disorders). Freud made great strides in redirecting medicine's focus back to respecting the mind's role in physical pain and illness. He believed that physical symptoms in the body represented emotional conflicts, usually based on repressed sexual desires.

Over the history of psychiatry, Freud's view of somatoform illness has been adapted and modified to the more common belief that somatoform disorders result from an individual's desire to keep traumatic, unpleasant, or disturbing experiences from conscious awareness. For example, in chapter one you read about Kevin, who experiences phantom-limb pain after losing his leg in military service. According to common psychiatric theory, a doctor might say that Kevin's body is manifesting physical pain to redirect Kevin's at-

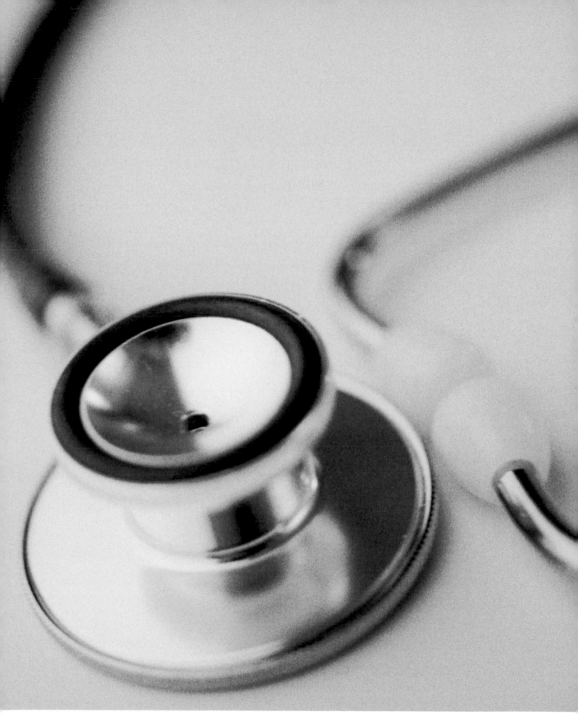

A somatoform disorder is often difficult to diagnose. It cannot be detected simply by listening through a stethoscope!

Drug Approval

Before a drug can be marketed in the United States, it must be officially approved by the Food and Drug Administration (FDA). Today's FDA is the primary consumer protection agency in the United States. Operating under the authority given it by the government, and guided by laws established throughout the twentieth century, the FDA has established a rigorous drug approval process that verifies the safety, effectiveness, and accuracy of labeling for any drug marketed in the United States.

While the United States has the FDA for the approval and regulation of drugs and medical devices, Canada has a similar organization called the Therapeutic Product Directorate (TPD). The TPD is a division of Health Canada, the Canadian government department of health. The TPD regulates drugs, medical devices, disinfectants, and sanitizers with disinfectant claims. Some of the things that the TPD monitors are quality, effectiveness, and safety. Just as the FDA must approve new drugs in the United States, the TPD must approve new drugs in Canada before those drugs can enter the market.

tention away from the trauma he experienced in Kosovo and his sorrow at losing a limb. His body does this in an attempt to protect Kevin from overwhelming emotional suffering. The psychosomatic physical symptoms become both a symbol of and a substitute for the unresolved emotional difficulties the patient has not faced.

Not everyone who experiences psychosomatic symptoms consistent with somatoform disorders has experienced something as traumatic and identifiable as war. Some people may develop somatoform disorders in response to generally stressful, fast-paced lifestyles or difficulties with interpersonal relationships. In North American society today, the term "stress-related disorders" is practically a catchphrase. While many people and doctors once equated the terms "psychological" or "stress-related illness" with "hysterical" or "imagined illness," today society in general and the medical field in particular are beginning to understand that mental and emotional conditions can cause true physiological changes.

Somatoform disorders are often difficult to identify because their symptoms occur in many other types of illnesses. People with psychological disorders such as depression, anxiety disorder, obsessive-compulsive disorder, and bipolar disorder often experience the same symptoms as individuals with somatoform disorders. When a person with somatoform symptoms first seeks treatment, it may be difficult for the doctor to discover whether the person is suffering from a somatoform disorder or from somatoform symptoms resulting from a different type of disorder. However, sometimes physical medical conditions are mistaken for psychologically based somatoform disorders. This is what happened to Jacquelyn. This can happen because some physical conditions, such as multiple sclerosis, have very elusive symptoms that may be mistaken for psychosomatic symptoms.

For a long time, many doctors thought that the best way to deal with a patient suffering from a psychosomatic condition was to humor the patient by giving him benign treatments (such as placebos, injections of water, and over-the-counter painkillers). The theory

In some serious somatoform disorders, a person's symptoms might be so overwhelming that it is difficult to treat the underlying condition. The patient may be experiencing so much pain and illness that she cannot focus on altering her lifestyle to reduce the stress that triggers her pain and illness. Perhaps the overwhelming nature of her pain causes her doctor to focus on treating this symptom as well. If true healing is to begin, however, it is imperative that patients are properly diagnosed and that the cause of their illnesses are treated.

Think about what would happen if you broke a bone in your leg. Your leg would hurt, swell up, and have lots of bruising. Now imagine that you go to the doctor, and the doctor prescribes a powerful painkiller and sends you home. For a little while, your leg might feel better, but it is still broken. The doctor has only treated your symptom, but not your actual ailment, and the next time you try to walk, you will realize that your ailment is just as bad as it was before receiving treatment.

behind this type of practice was that if the patient feels sick because his mind believes he is sick, the patient will feel better if his mind believes he is receiving treatment. Another reason that doctors participated in this type of "fake" treatment was because they thought the patient's psychosomatic symptoms were caused by a simple desire for attention. In giving benign treatments, some doctors believe they are providing the patient with the attention he is seeking while avoiding the uncomfortable and perhaps anxiety-producing inquiry into why the patient is seeking attention in the first place.

Most doctors now recognize that this is an inappropriate way to treat somatoform disorders. This type of "humoring" patients is inappropriate not only because it can be demeaning to the patient but also because it overlooks the true causes of these disorders. Furthermore, doctors may get caught up in focusing on treating symptoms rather than treating the disorder.

Pain and illness, seen as elements of the physical body alone, have historically been considered a subject for the medical field. But somatoform disorders like somatization disorder and pain disorders have shown us that biomedicine and rationalism do not hold the keys to all types of illnesses. In more recent times, there has been a push within the medical field and in academia to understand pain and illness as results of both the body and the mind. This drive has led scholars to explore more holistic views of the mind and body, allowing for the belief that legitimate pain and illness can occur within a person even without a readily identifiable physical cause.

holistic: Involving or focusing on the whole rather than the parts.

Clearly, the body and mind are intertwined. For example, the individual experiencing mental distress will, in all likelihood, display physical signs of this distress, such as sweating, an increased heart rate, or a forehead puckered in concentration. If severe enough, mental stress will often be accompanied by actual physical pain, such as the ache of the tensed shoulder muscles, the debilitating headache that just won't go away, or even the serious burning ulcer that refuses to be soothed. The medical field is currently expanding consideration for all types of treatments for somatoform disorders, including psychiatric counseling, group therapy, "alternative" means of pain and illness management, and drug therapy.

The death of a loved one can be so traumatic that it leads to a psychiatric disorder.

Chapter Three

How Some Psychiatric Drugs Work

Mauri had made his way to the grave site every day for the last two years. There, surrounded by silent stones, he sat with his wife. Sometimes he brought flowers or pictures of their children. Sometimes he spoke to his wife, telling her the newest events in world affairs, relating the latest troubles with the kids, or giving her updates on his poor health. But mostly, Mauri just sat as silent as the stones.

When Mauri's wife died, part of him seemed to die with her. That first day in the cemetery, watching her coffin as it was lowered into the dark cold ground, Mauri had wished he could descend into the darkness with her. He wanted to be lowered into that smothering blackness where he would not feel or hear or see his pain. If he too were buried in the earth, he would not need to know what life without her would be like—how difficult and joyless it would be.

When Roz was alive, she and Mauri were social, fun- loving people. They were active members of their synagogue; they hosted the best dinner parties of any of their friends. Roz organized fund-raisers for local charities. But when Roz died, all the joy and laughter stopped. Synagogue members, family, and close friends gathered around Mauri. His oldest daughter spent the first month after Roz's death living at the house, trying to help Mauri adjust to being on his own. When she went back to her own family, friends began bringing him warm meals and inviting him to their homes. But despite everyone's best efforts to make him feel better, Mauri withdrew. He didn't want their help, he didn't want their charity, but most of all he didn't want to be happy ever again. What was the point of happiness if he couldn't share it with Roz?

A year after his wife's death, Mauri's daughter cast an insult upon him that he did not think he could bear. When she came for her Saturday evening visit, she brought a woman along. Her name was Beth, and she was a widow Mauri's age. Her husband had died two years before. Mauri knew immediately what his daughter was trying to do, and it enraged him. "Why would you bring a perfect stranger here?" he demanded of his daughter.

"I thought you two might have a lot to talk about," his daughter replied. "Beth and Mom used to work together on the charity fund-raisers, and Beth also knows what it's like to lose the person you planned to grow old with. Dad, Mom's been dead for a year, and sooner or later you have to start moving on with your life."

To Mauri, this was the ultimate insult. Why would he want to move on? Roz was the best thing that had ever happened to him. They had raised children together and gotten older together. How did his daughter expect him to move on? He was furious with his daughter and told her that if she could not respect his wishes, his way of dealing with his loss, then she needn't come to see him anymore.

After spending a lifetime together, spouses may be unable to move on emotionally when one of them dies.

Soon after the confrontation with his daughter, Mauri's health began to deteriorate. He started losing weight and dark circles grew beneath his eyes. He felt his vision weakening and switched to stronger prescription glasses. He moved about slowly, every joint aching, and felt pains in his stomach and chest. Before, Mauri had simply refused friends' invitations to dinner and other social outings, but now he simply felt too sick to go, and in a way this excuse was a relief to him. His daughter and son-in-law were alarmed by his sudden change in health, but Mauri refused to see a doctor. In his daily visits to the cemetery, he began telling Roz that he was sure he would be

We all have seasons in our life, times of joy and times of loss. Antidepressants cannot change that normal cycle.

A common myth about antidepressants is that these drugs make you happy all the time. Antidepressants do not give a person "happy" chemicals, thereby removing all the downs the person might feel. Instead, antidepressants work by adjusting the balance of chemicals in a person's brain. However, the chemical balance in our bodies is constantly changing in response to numerous environmental, physical, and emotional factors. In the course of a day, you will feel many different sensations and emotions. You may be angry one moment, frightened the next, and laughing just a little while later. You may feel tired for an hour, and then have a surge of energy. These ups and downs are normal and necessary. But some people have a chemical imbalance that causes their emotional ups and downs to be severe and debilitating. Antidepressants work to bring the body's own chemicals into a healthy balance so that the person's daily experiences of highs and lows are within a normal range. It takes time for this balance to be achieved, and it is usually a number of weeks before an antidepressant medication has a significant effect on a person's depressive mood.

with her soon. "What a relief to everyone," he would say. "I will no longer be a burden to them or to myself. I look forward to the day."

But then one day everything changed, and Mauri was suddenly given something to live for. He had come home from visiting Roz's grave to find the green light blinking on his answering machine. He hit play and half listened as he slowly pulled off his boots. It was his daughter's voice speaking from the machine.

"Look, Dad," she said hesitantly, "I know we haven't gotten along well lately, but I just got home from the doctor, and I wanted you to be the first to know." Then she paused.

Mauri looked up at the answering machine as his heart flew into his throat. He was sure something horrible was about to happen. She was at the doctor; she was sick. Maybe she was dying. First Roz and then his daughter; a million horrible thoughts flew through his mind in the space of a second. Then his daughter's voice began again.

"I know that we haven't had a lot of joy in a long time, but I hope you can find some happiness in this. I'm pregnant. You're going to be a grandfather."

The message ended, and Mauri was flooded with a sense of relief and joy he had not experienced in years. He stepped back into his boots and went immediately back to the cemetery. He sat to tell Roz the good news; they were going to be grandparents. But as he spoke, the deep waves of depression began to break over him again as he thought about how much Roz had wanted grandchildren and how she would never get to see them. He knew, though, that Roz would want him to be there for their grandchild, to be a source of joy, comfort, and wisdom for this new young soul. Sitting there, wrapped in despair when he should be feeling joy, Mauri vowed to his wife that he was going to get better. He was going to spend time with their daughter and take care of his health. He would tell his grandchildren about their grandmother and what a wonderful person she had been.

But he knew he needed help; he was too sick to simply make himself well. Despite the obvious changes in Mauri's body, his doctor found nothing to account for his quick physical deterioration. "I could have told you that," Mauri said to his doctor. "The only thing that's wrong with me is a broken heart. But how do you fix that?"

The doctor gave Mauri a sympathetic smile, saying that the best healer could only be time. However, the doctor explained that sometimes, when a person suffers a great loss, his grief can escalate into a clinical depression and that taking an antidepressant medication might help. Furthermore, the doctor said that one of the most important steps in understanding and dealing with our emotions is to discuss them with other people. Mauri had isolated himself from all the people who could help him work through his pain. The doctor suggested that Mauri begin speaking with a psychologist or other person trained in counseling for the grieving process.

Brand Names vs. Generic Names

Talking about psychiatric drugs can be confusing, because every drug has at least two names: its "generic name" and the "brand name" that the pharmaceutical company uses to market the drug. Generic names come from the drugs' chemical structure, while drug companies use brand names to inspire public recognition and loyalty for their products.

Here are the brand names and generic names for some common psychiatric drugs:

- Ativan®   lorazepam
- Haldol®   haloperidol
- Klonopin®   clonazepam
- Paxil®   paroxetine hydrochloride
- Prozac®   fluoxetine hyrdrochloride
- Valium®   diazepam
- Xanax®   alprazolam
- Zoloft®   sertraline hydrochloride

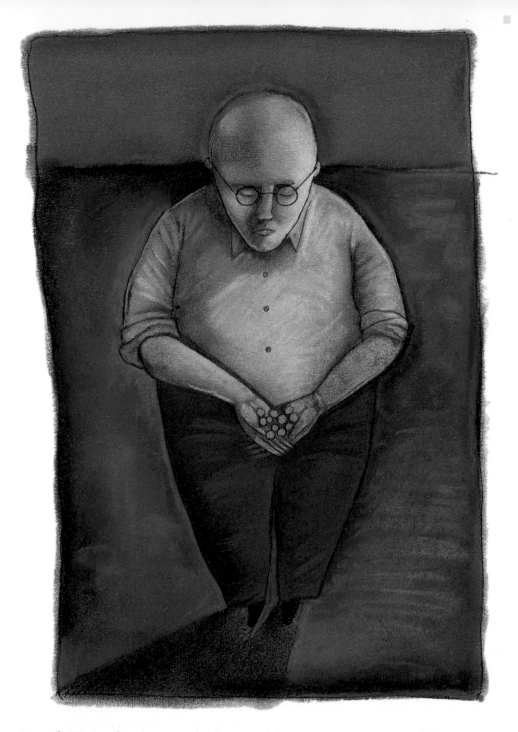

Psychiatric drugs may help an older person cope with his grief after the death of a loved one.

Mauri took the doctor's advice; he not only attended individual counseling, but he attended family counseling with his daughter and son-in-law as well. He was suspicious, however, of the antidepressant his doctor had prescribed. After all, how was a little pill going to make him feel better that his wife had died? But when he thought about the grandchild who would arrive in a few months, he was willing to try just about anything.

Many days, Mauri still had to struggle just to get out of bed in the morning, but after taking the pills for six weeks, he found that the struggle was getting easier. The aching in his joints grew less, his stomach no longer bothered him when he ate, and the horrible pain in his chest began to subside. He even found that he looked forward to the family counseling sessions where he could talk about his feelings and spend time with his daughter.

It was wonderful to look forward to something again. Then one morning, several months after his treatment began, Mauri woke to a phone call from his daughter. Mauri snatched the picture of Roz from his dressing table and tucked it into his pocket. Feeling like a new man, he ran to his car. That morning, instead of turning toward the cemetery, Mauri drove to the hospital to see his new grandchild.

Discussion

It may be easy to understand why somatoform disorders, which have a psychological basis, respond well to psychological treatments such as talk therapy. However, in Mauri's story we see that an important part of his treatment was antidepressant medication.

Patients with psychosomatic disorders experience a great range of symptoms, and a great range of psychiatric medications treats these symptoms. Because no drugs treat psychosomatic disorders directly, it is impossible to speak of any specific drug and its treatment of somatoform disorders. However, the general category of medications that seems to be most helpful for somatizing patients are the selective serotonin reuptake inhibitors (SSRIs), which include drugs such as Paxil, Prozac, and Zoloft. These drugs are normally used to treat depression and anxiety.

When prescribing medication, a doctor should consider the patient's individual symptoms carefully so as to prescribe the most beneficial drug. For example, a person with a somatoform disorder often suffers from depressive symptoms, so a psychiatrist may wish to prescribe an antidepressant. However, people with somatoform disorders also often have a very high level of daily anxiety. This should be considered carefully when choosing an antidepressant, because some antidepressants, like Wellbutrin, can have anxiety-producing side effects.

SSRIs are the most commonly prescribed antidepressants. Having too little serotonin in our bodies can affect our moods, sleep, eating habits, learning, and many other important functions. In some people, the cells that produce serotonin begin to reabsorb the serotonin before it can go out and perform its job in the body. SSRIs keep the cells from reabsorbing the serotonin and allows the serotonin to stay in the body longer, hopefully leading to an increase in serotonin levels and an improvement in the patient's quality of life. The SSRIs are often a good choice for patients with somatoform disorders because these antidepressants have a low incidence of anxiety-producing side effects.

A class of psychiatric drugs known as benzodiazepines, including Ativan, Xanax, Klonopin, and Valium, might be prescribed to a patient for anxiety. Unlike antidepressants, benzodiazepines work quickly to produce a calming effect, so they can be useful in helping a person in an immediate crisis situation. However, when prescribing medications to patients with somatoform disorders, doctors tend to avoid benzodiazepines because these drugs can be addictive. In certain cases, such as when a patient experiences severe acute-onset somatization in response to a traumatic event, the use of a benzodiazepine like Valium may be appropriate. Benzodiazepines are frequently used short term until an SSRI becomes effective and for "breakthrough" anxiety as needed.

The FDA bases its approval on specific research results. Sometimes, a particular use for a drug may have been thoroughly researched by many studies, while other uses lack the same amount of research. In that case, the drug label will only include the uses that have met the FDA's stringent research requirements. Physicians, however, may continue to prescribe that drug for other "off-label" uses. For instance, according to the labels found on beta-blockers, these medicines are approved for treating high blood pressure; medical practitioners, however, commonly prescribe beta-blockers for psychiatric uses.

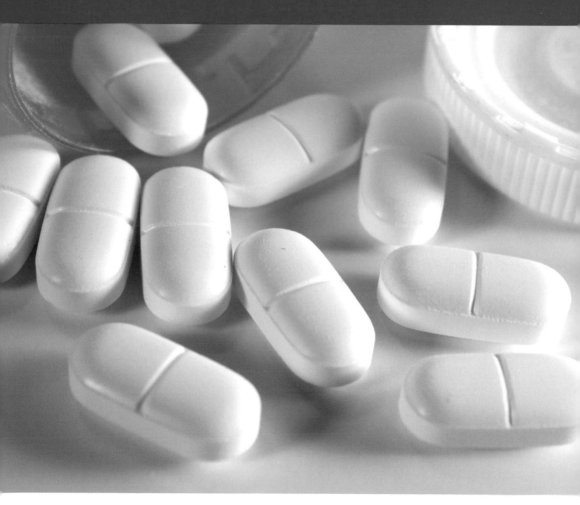

If you experience intense fear while watching a scary movie, your body will send out a burst of adrenaline, preparing you physically to cope with danger.

Adrenaline is the same hormone that floods wild animals' bodies when they are under attack. This hormone gives them a sudden burst of strength that can mean the difference between life and death. When a human being is under stress, adrenaline levels also rise. If adrenaline levels in a person stay high, the person will have difficulty functioning in normal situations because the brain has turned off its thinking functions, and the body has turned on to fight or run. Adrenaline levels in the body are good examples of how mental and emotional influences can produce dramatic physical effects in the body.

Like benzodiazepines, beta-blockers are also used in treating anxiety. They block adrenaline, which the body naturally produces in response to anxiety-provoking situations. The release of adrenaline causes the heart rate to rise, muscles to be flooded with blood and oxygen, and energy to surge. If a person is in danger, this flood of energy is vital so the person can protect himself or escape. But if these hormones remain at high levels for long periods of time, they could cause negative symptoms consistent with those seen in somatizing patients. Beta-blockers help to control this flood of adrenaline.

Many in the scientific community now believe that emotional stress and trauma can affect brain chemistry. No one, however, is quite sure how this happens. Nevertheless, this may be the reason why so many people with somatoform disorders also suffer from coexisting disorders like depression, anxiety, and eating disorders and respond well to medications that treat these disorders. Even though the somatoform disorders themselves are psychological disorders, the coexisting disorders sometimes have chemical or physical causes. The mind and body work together in complicated ways, and psychological conditions can produce physical changes that warrant medicinal treatment.

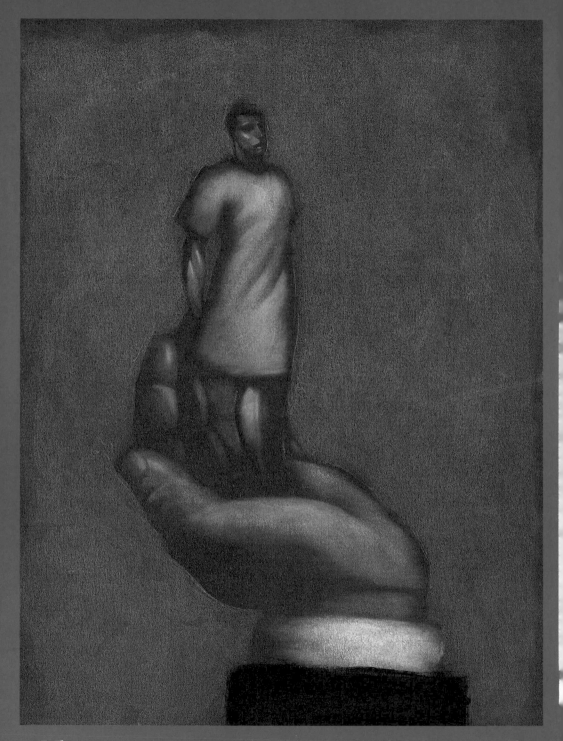

When a person enters psychiatric treatment, he places himself in the medical practitioner's hands. The medical practitioner has been trained to determine the best possible therapy for each individual.

Chapter Four

Treatment Description

On her first day of treatment, Kam Chi entered the unfamiliar office and allowed her eyes to drift slowly around the room, alighting on objects, noting the titles on the bookshelves, and regarding everything with a good deal of skepticism. Her gaze floated distantly over the brown leather couch. The dark leather reflected a deep red glow in the office's soft lighting. The thick area rug was woven with matching shades of red and brown. Here and there some yellow threads added warmth to the woven design. It all seemed very comfortable and pleasant, but Kam Chi wasn't convinced. She let out a quietly mocking sigh when she saw the tissues placed strategically on the table next to the couch. The white tissues rose out of a beautifully painted wooden box, as if they were an artistic focal point of the room.

This was stupid. Sure everything seemed soft and inviting, but how was it going to make her headaches, sore muscles, fatigue, and back spasms go away? "I need a doctor, not a therapist," Kam Chi muttered under her breath. She turned to leave and collided with a woman as she strode through the open door.

"You must be Kam Chi." The woman smiled. "I'm Dr. Ryan, and I'm so glad to meet you. Why don't you have a seat?"

Great, I'm trapped, Kam Chi thought. She gave a last wistful look at the door as Dr. Ryan eased it shut. As Kam Chi sank into the psychiatrist's leather couch, she was surprised by its softness. It seemed to reach up around her. After a moment, she gave in, allowing the couch to envelop her aching back. As long as she was here, she might as well try to enjoy it.

"Well, let's begin," Dr. Ryan smiled. "Why don't you tell me what brought you here."

Kam Chi began giving a list of her past physical ailments and current bodily complaints. She had given this history so many times before that she barely listened to what she was saying. These appointments were always the same, trying to rattle off as many symptoms as she could before the doctor interrupted her with his diagnosis and sent her on her way with a medication that wouldn't do any good.

Kam Chi had been speaking for fifteen minutes when she realized that Dr. Ryan hadn't interrupted her once. She stopped and waited. Dr. Ryan appeared to be waiting, too.

"Go on," the doctor encouraged after a moment.

"I think that's it," Kam Chi replied, somewhat surprised that she couldn't think of any other symptoms to report. "I think I've told you everything."

"Well, then." Dr. Ryan removed her glasses and turned to a new page in her notebook. "If it's all right with you, I have a few questions I'd like to ask. First, you've given me a good idea of your different physical symptoms. Can you tell me a bit about what else is going on in your life?"

Kam Chi was silent for a moment. "I don't think there's really that much to say."

Psychiatric disorders are often perceived as a trap. It may be difficult for a person to seek treatment, since she fears that she may end up in yet another trap she cannot escape.

"Just tell me about your daily life," Dr. Ryan encouraged. "I want to know how you spend your time—if you're in school or working, if you spend much time with your family, if you live by yourself or with other people. Things like that."

"There's really not much to tell. I'm in my senior year in high school. I really like school, and I have a lot of friends. I work hard to get good grades so that I can get into a good business school. I play the violin. I spend a lot of time with my parents. They're from China and don't speak English very well, so sometimes they need me to help them, you know, translating and stuff."

"That must be hard," Dr. Ryan commented.

"Not really. I grew up speaking Chinese at home, so I'm bilingual. I can switch back and forth between Chinese and English without even thinking."

"I meant it must be hard living with one culture, the Chinese culture, in your home and another culture, American culture, at school," Dr. Ryan replied.

"Oh, you bet it is." Kam Chi suddenly started speaking with urgency. "I mean, I love my parents, and it really makes me feel good that I can help them. But sometimes I feel pressured to be a good daughter. I just feel like they don't understand. Like the other day this guy at school asked me out on a date. I really like him. We've been friends for a long time, but I know that I can't date him because my parents are always talking about how wild American kids are, running around dating, partying, kissing—they see what's on TV and just think all American kids are like that. If I said I wanted to go on a date, they'd think I was like that, too. I know they want what's best for me, but I get frustrated too."

"It sounds like a lot of responsibility for someone your age. Kam Chi, do you think the stresses you are describing could have something to do with your health problems?"

Kam Chi thought for a moment. This was something she had never considered before. Was she stressed? She had never really thought of herself that way. She thought that she was just being responsible, doing what any good daughter would do. But now that

When a person is juggling many roles in life, stress may contribute to both emotional and physical health problems.

she thought about it, she often felt sick before having to do something important for her parents, like translating a conversation with a Realtor or going with them to have their taxes done. And she was definitely feeling more symptoms now she had started looking for colleges. "I don't know," Kam Chi said thoughtfully. "It's just that I've never really thought of myself as stressed. I don't feel panicked and anxious all the time. I'm just tired and have backaches and things."

"Well, Kam Chi," Dr. Ryan said, "not everyone experiences stress in the same way. Some people feel a lot of mental and emotional turmoil when they are under stress. But there are also people who internalize their stress. Perhaps they don't feel all of the emotional and mental side effects of their overworked lifestyles in their conscious mind, but they begin to feel physical side effects. They may

When a person is emotionally unaware of stress, she may experience it physically instead.

be engaged in a process known as somatization in which the person's body translates unresolved mental and emotional stresses into physical reactions like upset stomachs and aching muscles. We don't know enough yet to say for sure what is happening in your case, but what we do know is that you have a lot more responsibilities than most people your age. Furthermore, the approaches that you have taken thus far for dealing with your physical symptoms haven't been successful. These are big clues that stress may be causing a lot of your physical symptoms, and if that is the case, I think I can help you. Does that sound like something you'd be willing to consider?"

Kam Chi thought for a moment. She had entered Dr. Ryan's office with a lot of skepticism, but what the psychiatrist was saying seemed to make sense. She took a deep breath and met Dr. Ryan's smile. "What do I have to do?"

In today's world, many people are constantly battling time, trying to fit more into each hour. This leads to tension, which in turn can contribute to physical and emotional disorders.

Discussion

The fact that pain and illness have both physical and mental aspects suggests that individuals may be able through mental processes to regulate (or at the very least, cope with) the degree to which they experience pain and illness. Because somatoform disorders are thought to be caused by psychological conditions, psychiatric therapy is often used as a way to treat the psychological basis of the symptoms.

The first step doctors must take when treating somatizing patients is to recognize the patient's physical symptoms as legitimate

We cannot separate our bodies from our minds. Physical energy and emotional well-being are closely intertwined.

Some people believe that all pain and illness are "mind over matter." For example, there are cases in religious practices where individuals inflict what would be torture upon themselves, such as whipping themselves with leather straps, while apparently not feeling any pain. Some people claim to be able to walk over red-hot coals without feeling any pain. There are also examples of people having so much mental control over their physical bodies that they can regulate their heartbeat, blood pressure, and even their body temperature! These, of course, are very dramatic examples of "mind over matter." Psychiatric therapy, though less dramatic, encompasses a mind-over-matter approach to treating somatoform disorders; if the patient can gain control over her stress and emotions, she may be able to control her physical symptoms as well.

and approach the patient with a concerned and supportive attitude. The first step for patients in psychiatric therapy is to recognize that their somatic disorders are psychologically based and that the steps they have taken thus far in attempting to control their symptoms have not been helpful; a new approach is needed.

Psychotherapy is a very individual treatment, and each person's treatment plan will be different. Nevertheless, many therapists follow some helpful basic guidelines when creating a treatment program, regardless of the type of disorder for which the patient is being treated.

The first and most important step in therapy is to establish a secure environment for the patient. The therapist's office should be a place of trust where the patient feels encouraged to freely discuss physical and emotional matters that may be confusing, embarrassing, guilt inducing, frightening, or otherwise uncomfortable. The patient should feel both physically and emotionally safe.

Psychiatric therapy should provide the patient with a safe place where she can grow.

Defining and developing boundaries is another important step in beginning the treatment process. Many therapists believe there should be no physical contact between the doctor and the patient. Setting clear guidelines at the beginning of therapy regarding physical contact can help make the therapist's office a safe space. Therapists should also establish guidelines for telephone availability. Most therapists make themselves available by telephone for emergency situations only. Too much reliance on telephone conversation can have an adverse affect on the therapeutic doctor–patient relationship. If a patient calls her therapist every time she feels uncomfortable or confused, she will not learn how to deal with and overcome

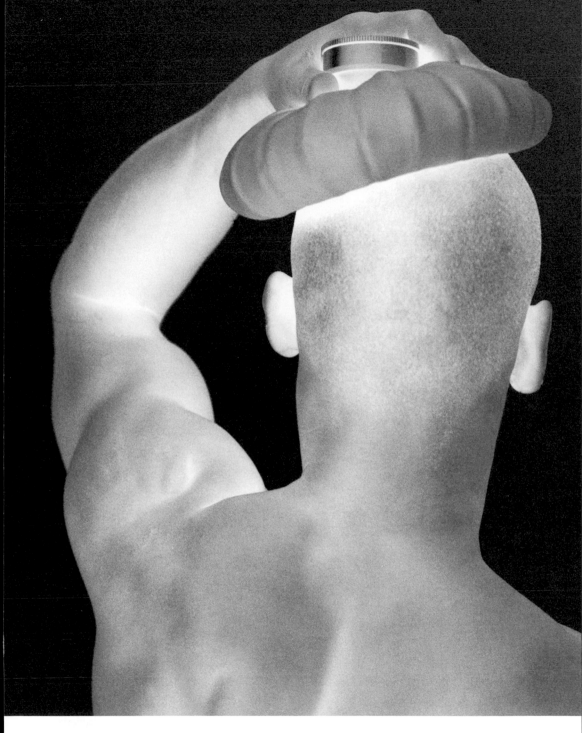

Physical pain that is caused by a psychiatric disorder is just as real as any other.

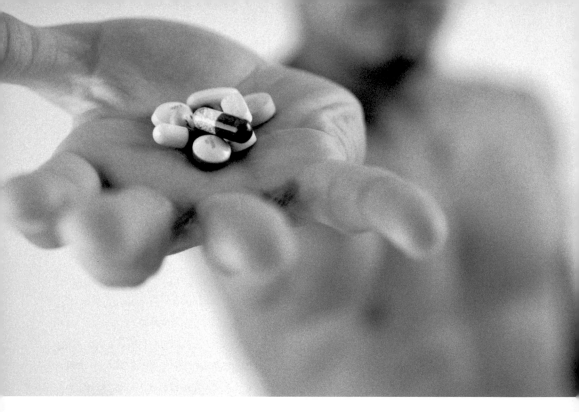

Medication is just one aspect of successful therapy for a person with a psychosomatic disorder.

difficulties on her own. Furthermore, since some somatoform disorders may be motivated by the patient's need for attention and affirmation, too much dependence on the doctor or therapist could make the patient's condition worse instead of better.

Treatment scheduling is also an important part of defining the boundaries of therapy. Most therapists see patients for one hour (or 50 minutes) each week. A regular treatment schedule is important so that the patient is able to deal with mental and emotional stressors as they arise. A regular schedule will also help the patient not become overly dependent on her doctor. Although psychiatric therapy can last a long time, even years, in most cases it is not meant to be a lifelong activity. Eventually, the patient will move beyond therapy, and when this happens the patient must know that she can maintain good mental health on her own without her therapist's help.

Once a safe place and boundaries for therapy have been established, the doctor and patient should discuss the goals of therapy. Over the course of treatment, patients and therapists should periodically review the goals of the treatment program. Checking in on goals can help patients determine if they are making progress. Additionally, the goals one begins with when starting therapy may change over time. One might realize that a specific goal is unreasonable for her time frame. However, one might find that she surpassed a goal long ago and that it is time to set new goals.

For most people with psychiatric disorders, therapy is a process that has both ups and downs. Sometimes a patient will make exciting progress, but there will probably also be frustrating relapses or backward steps. Expectations for therapy should be reasonable and flexible. Beginning treatment with the goal of eliminating all somatic symptoms is probably an unrealistic goal that will quickly lead to frustration and setbacks. Beginning therapy with the goal of recognizing things that trigger psychosomatic reactions and managing psychosomatic symptoms as they arise is a much more appropriate goal. Patients should understand that needing to alter goals or slow the pace of therapy is in no way a failure; it is simply an adjustment for their current needs.

Treatment for somatoform disorders does not just occur in the doctor's office. Some of the most important parts of patients' treatments happen outside of the medical environment. Doctors recommend that patients with somatoform disorders find ways to reduce the stress and feel more control in their daily lives. Stress-reducing activities often involve things like regular massages, learning deep breathing and meditation, creating artwork, and exercising. Regular exercise has been shown to be especially important for somatizing patients because it helps maintain health, provides a mental break from daily stresses and responsibilities, enhances self-esteem, and gives the patient a sense of control over her body and her body's functioning.

If a patient, in consultation with his doctor, decides that medication might be a helpful addition to his psychiatric therapy, he will have to follow the treatment program carefully. In the case of

Did you know that art can be therapeutic? Human beings have always used art to express the feelings inside of them. More and more therapists are finding that art can be an important part of therapy. Patients can often draw, paint, or use other artwork to express the feelings for which they don't have words. Many people also find the process of creating art to be calming, meditative, and therapeutic. For some patients, creating artwork helps them not only to express their feelings about a certain situation but also to soothe their emotions and calm their minds.

somatoform disorders, the doctor would probably begin by prescribing an SSRI. There are many SSRIs, and it would be up to the doctor to decide which of these medications to prescribe. Doctors usually begin by prescribing the medication that has the lowest rate of side effects. However, not every drug works for every person, so a patient may need to try a number of different drugs before finding the one that is right for him. Although some people feel relief within three weeks, it can take eight to ten weeks for psychiatric medications to begin taking effect.

Many psychiatric drugs require a build-up period—a period of time when the patient takes a smaller than average dose so that her body can get used to the medication. This may affect the amount of time it takes for the patient to experience any benefit from the drug. For example, the typical therapeutic dose for the SSRI Zoloft is fifty milligrams once each day. However, a patient who is just beginning to take Zoloft would generally begin by taking a twenty-five-milligram dose once each

therapeutic dose: The amount of medication that provides a positive effect for the patient. For example, a child would only need a small amount of Tylenol to treat her symptoms, but a therapeutic dose of Tylenol for an adult would require a much larger amount.

People with somatoform disorders often have coexisting disorders such as obsessive-compulsive disorder, depression, or anxiety. In some cases, patients are prescribed medications not for their somatoform disorder but for these coexisting disorders. It is important to remember that treating a coexisting disorder is not the same thing as treating the primary somatoform disorder. However, if the patient can bring her coexisting disorder under control with medication, she may be able to focus on her therapy and make greater strides in overcoming her somatoform disorder.

day so that her body can adjust to the medication. After one week, the dosage should be increased to fifty milligrams once each day. For some people, fifty milligrams of Zoloft is still too little to produce a therapeutic effect. In this case, the doctor would slowly increase the dosage up to a maximum of two hundred milligrams per day. The amount of time it takes for a patient's body to adjust to a therapeutic dose will affect how long it is before the patient notices any benefits from taking the medication.

Some people find that once they have learned to deal with the stress and emotions causing their somatoform disorders, they are able to proceed without medications; others may find that medications are a necessity in the ongoing maintenance of good health. For example, a patient with a conversion disorder might be able to reduce the stress in her life enough to reduce or even end her psychosomatic neurological symptoms but still have a coexisting mood disorder like depression that makes medication a necessary part of the rest of her life.

Many people, not just those with psychiatric conditions, live and thrive because of the help of medication. People with conditions such as severe asthma and diabetes must always take medication to maintain good health. Long-term medication for psychiatric conditions can be thought of in the same way.

A perfectionist may be driven to succeed in school. In Carmen's case, the constant pressure led to a psychsomatic disorder.

Chapter Five

Case Studies

The individuals who experience psychosomatic disorders are each unique. Many of them find that drug therapy helps them handle their symptoms—while for others, drug therapy will not offer the answers they need for their disorder.

A Case Study in Somatization Disorder

Carmen was a perfectionist, always had been, and thought she always would be. She could not tolerate the thought of not being the best; she was paralyzed by the thought of failure. Even in elementary school, she had been driven by the need to succeed and had terrible stomach cramps before tests. In middle school, she had always felt dizzy before soccer games. By the time she reached high school, her need to be perfect began to hold her back. Sometimes in class, she would be so afraid of answering a question incorrectly that she would not answer the question at all—even though she was sure she knew the answer! But it was years later, when Carmen began attending law school at McGill University, that things really started getting bad.

The first year of law school Carmen was so busy she barely paid attention to anything but her studies. She worked late into the nights and got up early in the mornings. She stopped exercising and barely had time to eat, let alone eat properly. By her second year, her life-style was beginning to take its toll. Carmen felt exhausted all the time and occasionally was too sick to go to class. Other symptoms troubled her as well—she had stopped menstruating, and she often had a sense that her heart was racing. She eventually made time to see numerous doctors, but they could find no reasonable explanation for her symptoms.

By the end of law school, Carmen realized she was barely making it through. Her grades had fallen, and she'd lost confidence in her abilities. As the date for the bar exam approached, Carmen began to feel weaker and sicker. Finally, she decided that with her health as fragile as it seemed to be, there was no way that she could be a good lawyer. How could people depend on her to represent them in court if she couldn't even depend on herself to be able to get out of bed in the morning? Carmen decided to not take the bar exam, and she became a legal secretary instead.

In the next ten years, Carmen saw her health decline into a self-perpetuating downward spiral. The worse she felt, the less she did—and the less she did, the worse she felt. In less than a decade, she watched her body decline from that of a strong twenty-three-year-old to what one

self-perpetuating:
Causing itself to continue.

would expect from a person who was sixty-five years old. But even worse than that, Carmen was plagued by feelings of failure. Her job was challenging and took a lot of legal knowledge, but every day she went to work feeling she had not lived up to her full potential. She had planned to be a lawyer. Now she ran errands and typed papers for lawyers. She resented being a subordinate to the lawyers, and she was depressed by her position.

On Carmen's thirty-fourth birthday, she woke and stared at the ceiling. Her apartment seemed so quiet and empty. She felt the aching of her muscles and thought about how much she dreaded getting out of bed. After all, what could this day possibly bring but sadness? All the other people she knew who were thirty-four were dating or already married. They weren't living in lonely apartments; they were buying houses and having children. They didn't seem depressed by their jobs; they were building careers and looking forward to futures with even better careers awaiting them. They didn't fall exhausted and aching into bed as soon as they got home from work; they went and played racquetball, went to see movies, or took their dogs for strolls in the park.

What was she doing? She looked around at the spiderwebs that had multiplied in the corners she could not reach to clean. She was thirty-four years old, she thought, and if she did not get out of this bed and make some changes in her life, she was going to die here in this room staring at these same cobwebs. She decided to get out of bed, and her birthday present to herself that year was a membership to the local health club.

Carmen's doctor was relieved to hear of her decision to begin exercising. They had spent years discussing the psychosomatic nature of her physical condition, but she had never taken a step like this one before. After ten years of working with Carmen, he had begun to think that a breakthrough like this one would never come. But she truly seemed to want to take control of her life, her health, her body, and her mind, and there was something contagious about her new enthusiasm to get well. They began working on a plan together.

A pet may provide unexpected emotional and physical benefits!

Despite Carmen's commitment to the plan, her doctor warned against too much too fast. He explained that she had a long road to wellness ahead of her and that trying to make up too much ground too fast could lead to frustration and possibly devastating setbacks. For the first time since she began seeing him, Carmen took her doctor's advice very seriously. He recommended that she begin exercising by taking a water aerobics class three times a week. He explained that water aerobics was low impact exercise and would help gently ease her into stretching and using her muscles again.

Carmen also found an unexpected benefit in that the classes provided a great social opportunity. In the classes she met many people like herself, people who had been away from exercise for a long time and were trying to get back into it. There were people who had suffered injuries and surgeries and used water aerobics as therapeutic exercise. She found other people's determination inspiring and saw some of the overwhelming obstacles that they faced. This made her even more determined to get well.

As Carmen's health improved, her confidence improved as well. After a number of months, she was able to move out of the pool to start some other exercise programs as well. She asked another member of the gym to show her how to lift weights to start building her strength. Walking past the park on her way home one day, she noticed the people playing with their dogs. The next day she decided to volunteer as a dog walker at the local animal shelter. At the shelter, an overweight dog named Shelby, who had been brought in with numerous health problems, became her special project. Each day, Carmen tried to walk a little further with Shelby than she had the previous day. Eventually, Carmen and Shelby both grew strong enough to go for short runs in the park.

Carmen also decided to go back to school. With the increased stress of classes, she began taking yoga in the morning. She found yoga to be a great way to relax and start her day with a clear mind. She brought Shelby home to live with her, and when Carmen had mornings when she felt like she couldn't get out of bed, Shelby would appear, tail thumping and leash in mouth, ready for their morning run. Carmen would pull herself out of bed, realizing that she felt

Do pets have healing powers? Some doctors say they do! Studies suggest that people who have pets may have fewer mental disorders, recover from illness and surgery faster, and stay healthier longer. Doctors believe that these health benefits result from the fact that pets are a source of unconditional love and comfort and that people who have pets feel like they have a reason to stay healthy. In Carmen's battle against somatization disorder, her dog Shelby gives her a reason to stay motivated. Shelby also brings a lot of happiness into Carmen's life. For a person with a somatoform disorder, the things that bring peace and well-being to the mind also bring well-being to the body. Pets can be especially important for elderly people and people who do not have family living close by. Some nursing homes have even begun bringing pets in to live among the residents. The vast majority of residents living in these homes report that having pets improves their quality of life.

better than she had in ten years, and that she and Shelby were going to get even better still.

Carmen was on her way to recovery. In her case, exercise and a new attitude had proved to be the therapy she needed. She had not needed to use psychiatric drugs at all.

A Case Study in Body Dysmorphic Disorder

Patrick Tompson was thrown into the harsh spotlight of fame when he was just seventeen years old. He had dreamed of being a singer, and at first, the rush of success was everything he had hoped for and more.

Patrick's single was at the top of the charts. Girls recognized him everywhere he went. Requests were pouring in from daytime talk shows for interviews and singing engagements. He could turn on the radio and hear himself singing back. All the attention he suddenly had was more than just exciting; it was powerful, intoxicating. He breathed it in as he breathed air. Every morning he walked to the newsstand and scoured the newspapers and magazines for reviews of his CD and talk of his upcoming performances. Nothing had prepared him for the nightmare that came along with his dream.

Patrick was engaged in his morning routine when he read a review that would stay with him forever. It said, "I've heard a lot about

Yoga can reduce stress and contribute to mental focus.

Many people in North American society think that only young girls are concerned about their looks and that disorders such as body dysmorphic disorder, anorexia, and bulimia only affect females. Studies, however, suggest that men suffer from body dysmorphic disorder as often as women do. However, the assumption in our society that only women suffer from such disorders may lead men to deny their conditions or may cause medical professionals to overlook a diagnosis of body dysmorphic disorder in men.

this Patrick Tompson lately, so I finally decided to see what all the fuss was about. I have to say, I was surprised." Patrick smiled, but his smile quickly faded as he read on. "With his crooked nose looking like he just stepped out of the boxing ring and his too-long hair looking like he took a time machine from the sixties—why Tompson is our newest teen heartthrob, this reviewer will never know."

Patrick had been warned that there are always bad reviews. He knew that he should stop reading right there, but he couldn't help himself. He plunged on. "Patrick Tompson offers nothing that is attractive to me, and his music isn't any better. But music fans, don't hang your heads in despair yet. Tompson won't be on the charts for long. He's no prizefighter and no Beatle. So my advice to everyone is this: close your eyes and plug your ears until the next one-hit wonder comes along."

Patrick was devastated. It wasn't the reviewer's comments about his music that bothered him so much. He had been studying voice and music since he was six years old, and he knew he was good. What really stuck with him was the reviewer's attack on his looks. Patrick went straight home and examined himself in the mirror. The reviewer was right: his nose was crooked. How could he have never noticed it before? Why had no photographer said anything before?

Men as well as women can become obsessed with body image.

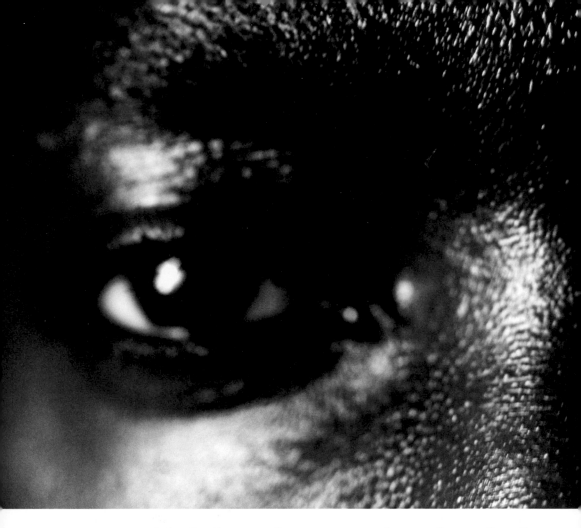

A person with body dysmorphic image may be so obsessed with some detail of his appearance that he becomes convinced that he is hideous as a result of some minor or even nonexistent flaw.

He had always liked his long hair, but now he thought the reviewer was right: it was too long. It didn't look hip and cool; it looked scraggly and dirty. He left immediately to see his hairstylist.

For the next year, the media praised Patrick's evolving image. His record label said he was maturing as an artist. No one but Patrick knew what was really going on. He was becoming obsessed with how he looked. People stared at him everywhere he went. He couldn't get away from their eyes. He began to believe that they looked at him not because he was famous but because he had a crooked nose. After a while, he began obsessing about other features as well—his eyes were too small, his lips looked deformed. He wondered if his mother had dropped him on his face when he was young. He thought the girls who fawned over his good looks were mocking him. He couldn't leave his house unless he looked perfect, and he was afraid to let one hair get out of place. He filled his house with mirrors until there were mirrors in every room and on every wall. As he moved through the house, he checked in the mirrors for any flaw that might have materialized. Some days he would check his reflection hundreds of times. Other days he would turn every one of the one hundred and three mirrors around to face the wall, or he would refuse to leave his room. He became reclusive, and yet somehow, the worse Patrick felt and the more reclusive he got, the more his fans grew to love him and the more young women talked about his "mysterious" side.

Patrick's career did not begin to suffer until his plastic surgery. When he decided to have plastic surgery on his nose, the media suddenly went crazy. Talk show hosts wanted to know what the surgery had been like. Tabloids ran articles speculating on Patrick's "secret life." Half his fans turned on him saying he'd become shallow and "out of touch." Patrick just sank deeper into despair, thinking that now he looked even worse than before. Soon he was having another surgery to correct the "mistake" of the last. And then he had another surgery after that. Four surgeries later, he realized that the facial alterations had also altered his voice. It wasn't bad, he knew, but it was not the voice he had before.

When Patrick finally admitted that he had a problem and that this problem was of his mind, not his nose, he sought psychiatric therapy. In therapy he began to realize that the pressure of stardom had been too much too young. He had not been prepared for how being in the constant public eye would affect him. His psychiatrist called his problem body dysmorphic disorder. Patrick began taking

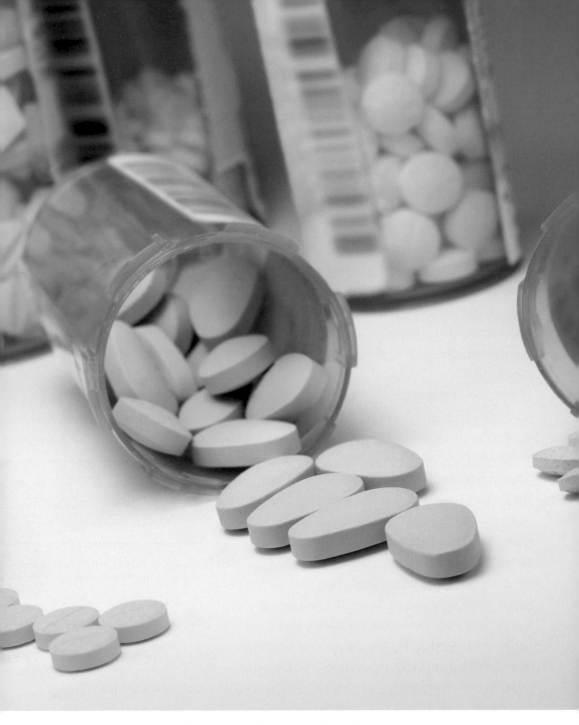

Antianxiety medication along with other therapy can help a person control an obsession with appearance.

an antianxiety medication in conjunction with his therapy. He found that this helped him to control his overwhelming obsession with his appearance and fear of being in public. Patrick realized that it was time for him to get out of the public eye, and so he left singing, embarking instead on a path toward healing.

A Case Study in Somatoform Disorder Not Otherwise Specified

Gillian's mother had died of a heart attack at the young age of forty. At that time, the medical field claimed that women weren't at risk for heart attacks, an opinion that everyone now knows is false. Gillian had always felt betrayed by this medical failure. Her mother hadn't known the warning signs. No one knew her mother was sick until it was too late.

The fact that her mother had died so young made Gillian acutely sensitive to changes in her own body. She exercised five times a week and was a vegetarian. Instead of driving to work, Gillian rode her bicycle. She took her vitamins and calcium supplements religiously. She always wore sunscreen outside. Gillian knew she was doing everything right, yet she couldn't get the number forty out of her mind.

Three months before Gillian's fortieth birthday, she began having heart palpitations. Fearing the worst, Gillian checked herself into the emergency room. The doctors found nothing to account for the slight arrhythmia but kept her overnight for observation, and then sent her home. But her peace of mind only lasted two days. Then Gillian felt tightness in her chest and a pain in her left arm. She returned to the emergency room.

> palpitations: Rapid, irregular, or pulsating beating of the heart.
>
> arrhythmia: Irregularity in heartbeat.

In Gillian's story we see how closely psychosomatic symptoms can mirror other medical conditions. Gillian has all of the symptoms of a heart condition with none of the physiological causes. Gillian's somatoform disorder is also an example of an acute-onset psychosomatic condition because her symptoms manifest quickly and severely. Like many acute-onset somatoform conditions, Gillian's symptoms also end as quickly as they appeared.

EKG (electrocardiogram): A test of the electrical currents of heart muscle activity used to detect heart abnormalities.

ultrasound: A test that uses ultrasonic waves to create an image of an internal body structure.

When Gillian explained her symptoms and the fact that her mother had died of a heart attack at the age of forty, the doctors suddenly took her concerns more seriously. They told her she was right to come in, that heart disease has a strong hereditary component. But even after a thorough workup, Gillian's lab results showed nothing. Her EKG was normal. An ultrasound of the arteries in her neck showed no plaque or congestion of the artery walls. Her cholesterol was low.

Gillian continued having these symptoms until the date of her fortieth birthday. After that day, her symptoms disappeared as mysteriously as they had come. When the doctor saw how quickly Gillian's symptoms subsided, he said he thought he now knew what she had been suffering from. He called it a somatoform disorder not otherwise specified. He explained to Gillian that he thought her symptoms had been brought on by an emotional crisis within herself. Her mother's death at forty had planted a deep-rooted fear in Gillian that the same thing would happen to her. She feared this possibility so much that as age forty approached, her body began producing the feared symptoms. Once her fortieth birthday passed, however, Gillian realized that she would not die as her mother had, and with her new peace of mind, her symptoms subsided.

Summary

There are no simple answers for people who experience psychosomatic disorders. For some, drug treatment can help them live productive and pain-free lives; for others, drug therapy will not be the answer. Nearly all will also need ongoing supplemental therapy (counseling and behavioral therapy, for example). These various treatment programs, often combined, give help and hope to individuals who struggle with psychosomatic disorders.

Traumatic events can trigger psychosomatic and other psychiatric disorders. Although in many cases, psychiatric medication can help, side effects should always be carefully monitored.

Chapter Six

Risks and Side Effects

David was on the phone with his wife when the Twin Towers fell outside his window. He watched in shock and horror as the massive buildings came crumbling down in slow motion, each story bursting below the next, like sifting sand. The telephone line went dead as he watched the structure disintegrate into dust, and he held his breath as the dust billowed toward and enveloped his office window. The whole world shook, and he was suddenly alone in the cloud, afraid that his building would fall next.

After that day, death accosted him everywhere—first immediate and mind-numbing, present in the bleeding people on the street, the graphic footage on the news, and the doomsday-gray dust that coated everything. Then came the endless funerals for the people who had been found and the memorials for the people who had not.

Fourteen of his friends had died that day, and each of their funerals made him feel more fragile and alone. After the funerals, the presence of death became subtler. Now death crept up in the whispered talk of war, sinister anthrax scares, and the rumors of hidden terrorist plots and cells. Death seemed to always be lurking just around the corner. Every day on his way to work, he passed Ground Zero, where the groan of machinery was never ending, an ever-present reminder of how everything went to pieces that September day.

Soon David could not bear going to work. It wasn't just the memories, which flooded him every time he walked down the street. It was the fumes as well. The smell of dust and death, of crushed cement and scorched metal clung to everything. His lungs burned with it. His head reeled with it. His stomach ached with it. He could not eat his lunch without throwing up. He became convinced that the air was contaminated, that there was something even more deadly on those planes that was now slowly killing them all.

David requested a transfer out of the city, but even in his new job in upstate New York, his fears grew. He was no longer afraid of toxic fumes, but now his fears turned to anthrax, then polio, then smallpox. He listened to talk of biological warfare on the nightly news. Each news story reaffirmed David's belief that he had been and was still being contaminated with something deadly.

David began seeing his doctor for the smallest complaints. He was sure every cough or minor skin irritation was the precursor to disaster. He demanded numerous blood tests and X rays. He wanted to be screened for every possible disease. He knew that his doctor was correct when he told David that his requests were expensive and unreasonable. Despite knowing that his fears were excessive, David still could not feel reassured.

Eventually, his doctor diagnosed him with hypochondriasis and post-traumatic stress disorder. He prescribed an antidepressant, but David's anxiety seemed to increase, a side effect that antidepressants sometimes cause. David and his doctor next tried antianxiety medications as well, but these too soon failed. It seemed that as soon as David began showing a positive response to his medications,

Psychiatric drugs are expensive—and they may carry other hidden costs as well.

Psychiatric drugs should never be taken casually, the way one might treat a stomachache or headache.

a sudden deluge of negative side effects would descend. His doctor began to believe that if a possible side effect to a given medication existed, David would develop it.

David and his doctor both had to concede that pharmacological treatment was not the right one for him.

Discussion

An unfortunate complication of somatoform disorders is that many patients with psychosomatic symptoms seem to also be hypersensitive to the negative side effects of medication. Psychiatric medications like antidepressants hold much hope for treating somatoform disorders. Unfortunately, negative side effects can make such drugs impossible for some patients to tolerate.

Psychiatric drugs have a wide range of side effects. They can cause anything from nausea, to sleeplessness, to severe neurological dysfunctions like seizures. Some of the most common side effects of SSRIs include somnolence (sleepiness, drowsiness, or fatigue), nausea,

hypersensitive: Reacting more intensely than most people.

diarrhea, and vomiting. Many psychiatric and other types of drugs cannot be mixed with alcohol, aspirin, over-the-counter drugs, or other medications. For some psychiatric medications, something as seemingly simple as having a glass of wine with dinner or taking an over-the-counter cold medication could produce serious, even life-threatening effects. Patients must be very careful to discuss these issues with a doctor before they begin taking medication.

Side effects can happen for many reasons and do not necessarily mean that a person should stop taking her medication. Some side effects are a sign that the dosage of medication is too high. Lowering the dosage might eliminate the side effects while still providing therapeutic benefits. Other side effects may be temporary—something that the patient feels while her body adjusts to the medication but that will go away with time.

When women take psychiatric medications, they should first carefully consider how these drugs may interact with hormones. Some drugs may make women become less fertile, decreasing the likelihood that they will become pregnant, while other drugs may hinder the action of birth control pills. Becoming pregnant while taking a psychiatric medication can be dangerous, since these drugs can affect the development of the baby.

Patients with somatoform disorders, however, often suffer psychosomatic side effects to taking their medications. Just as the patient's physical condition is being caused by the patient's mind, so too are side effects like those caused by the patient's mental reaction to the drug rather than the body's physiological reaction to the drug. For example, a patient may read a story about a person who became terribly sick when taking a certain medication. When the doctor prescribes this medication for her, she may be so afraid of getting this illness that her brain actually convinces her body she is sick, even though the drug did not make her ill.

This is what happens to David. David already imagines that he has or fears that he will get all the illnesses he hears about in the media. He reacts to the side effects of medications in the same way, either imagining or actually manifesting these symptoms.

Besides the possibility of having psychosomatic reactions to one's medication, other risk factors should also be taken into consideration. For example, women planning to take psychiatric medications should consider the effects these drugs might have on fertility and pregnancy. Some psychiatric drugs affect hormone levels in the body, thereby reducing fertility rates. On the other hand, many psychiatric drugs interact with birth-control pills, causing them to lose their effectiveness, increasing the woman's chance of becoming pregnant. This can be very dangerous, because many of these same drugs can also be toxic to the developing fetus. In some cases, psychiatric drugs may have caused conditions such as spina bifida, heart abnormalities, and neurological defects. The vast majority of women taking psychiatric drugs are able to have normal pregnancies and deliver healthy babies, but the benefits and risks of taking medication during pregnancy should always be considered carefully before becoming pregnant. Furthermore, many drugs can be transferred to a baby through the mother's breast milk, so a

spina bifida: A birth defect characterized by exposure of a portion of the spine.

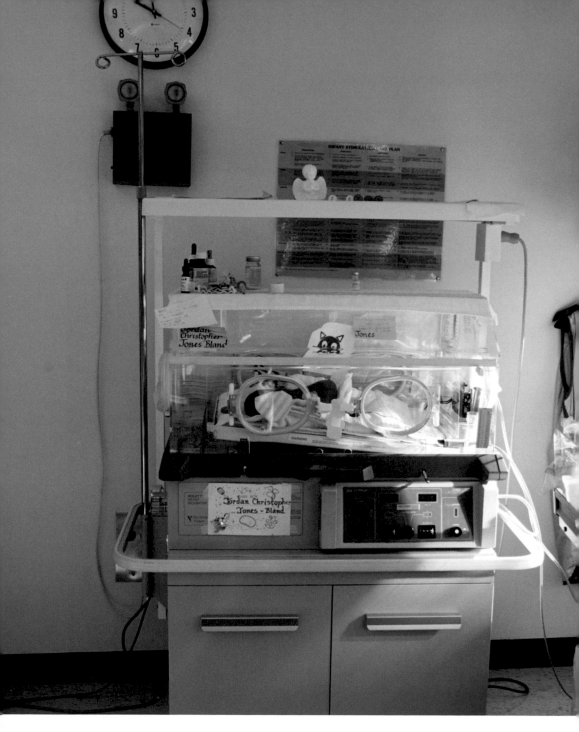

In some cases, psychiatric drugs have contributed to high-risk births.

new mother who is on psychiatric medications may be unable to breast feed.

In some instances, side effects force a person to stop taking medication, but ceasing medication can also be a complicated process. Stopping medication suddenly can produce negative and dangerous side effects of its own. A doctor should counsel a patient on whether her specific medication can be discontinued immediately or if she needs to taper off slowly. The risks and side effects associated with each particular psychiatric drug can also be found in *The Physicians' Desk Reference*.

Everything we put into our bodies has an effect. Most things, we hope, will have a positive effect. For example, food gives us energy. Water hydrates us. Air provides oxygen to our cells. Unfortunately, other things can have negative effects. Eating peanuts can give energy to one person but can be fatal to a person with a severe peanut allergy. One person may swallow chlorinated water while swimming and feel fine. Another person may swallow the same amount of chlorinated water and feel sick. Medications also have both positive and negative effects. For some people, like David, the negative effects of medication may be so severe that they outweigh any positive gains. Other people, however, may experience only the positive effects of a given medication.

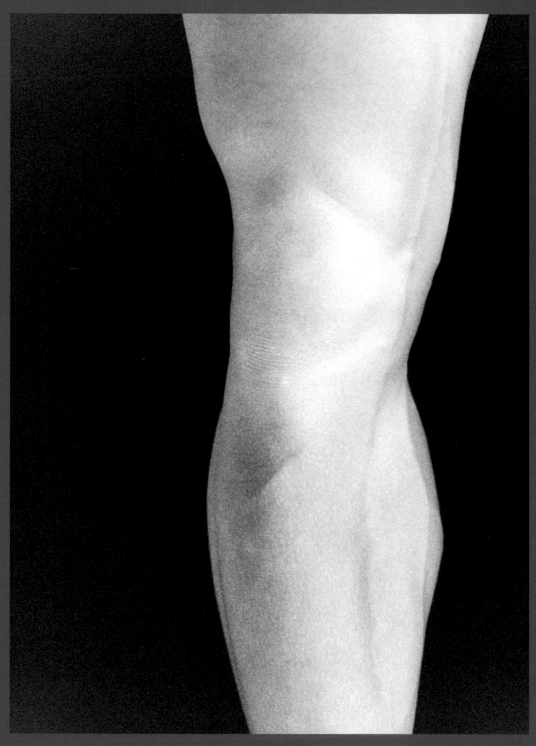

A person's amputated leg may continue to seem very real. It will often seem to itch or throb with pain, even though it is no longer there.

Chapter Seven

Alternative Treatments and Therapies

K evin sometimes claims that the Internet saved his life. He says this because it was through the Internet that he found the members of his support group. Since meeting them, he has begun to regard the loss of his leg and the pain he still feels in a whole new way.

After returning from Kosovo, every therapy, medicine, and painkiller had failed Kevin. Over the years, the pain in his leg and the nightmares while he slept grew worse, until he thought that perhaps he'd rather die than live like this. That is when, in desperation, he turned to the Internet for help. What he had done was a desperate shout in the dark. He posted a note that stated simply, "I am a

People who serve in the armed forces and homeland security are often called on to face great danger. Their bravery sometimes carries enduring costs.

former soldier and an amputee. I don't think I can live with this phantom pain any longer. Can't anybody help?"

He never expected the tremendous response he had gotten. He received e-mails from all over North America. They came from doctors, therapists, family members of amputees, other soldiers, and amputees like himself. All of them offered helpful advice and related stories that showed him he was not alone. But there were three e-mails that stood out from all the others. Each was from a person like himself, someone who had suffered an amputation in the line of duty and who now lived with phantom-limb pain. Most surprising of all, each person lived within a few hours' driving distance of Kevin's home.

The first of the three e-mails had come from a man named Rory. Rory was Kevin's age and lived in Toronto. He had been a firefighter who was rescuing a child from a house fire when a burning support beam came crashing down upon him. Miraculously, his fellow firefighters saved him and the child, but the doctors were not able to save his arm. That was five years ago, but the pain and burning had never left his phantom limb.

The second e-mail came from Kara, a woman in Buffalo, New York. She had been an active duty police officer, but now had to work behind a desk. She and her partner had been shot at the scene of a convenience store robbery. Her partner fell first, and she opened fire on the shooter, killing him before she kneeled beside her partner as he too died. Mind and heart numb, she did not realize that she had been shot until reaching the hospital. Just a flesh wound, and everyone thought she would be fine—physically at least—until a **staph** infection set in that eventually claimed her leg. Now she also suffered the same pain that Kevin suffered.

staph: A serious, potentially fatal, infection caused by the bacteria staphylococcus.

The third e-mail came from Donald, a man whom the others in the group would all grow to look up to as if he was their father. In his early eighties, he was a World War II veteran. He lost both of his legs on the beaches of Normandy and spent most of the rest of his life learning to live a full and happy life—despite horrible physical and emotional pain.

Taking a leap of faith, Kevin wrote to these three people who seemed to have so much in common with him, asking if they would like to get together in person. In their very first meeting, everyone knew that Kevin had started something special. It was so good to talk with other people who understood the physical and emotional pain they lived with every day. And each member of the group brought different perspectives and ideas for dealing with their pain.

A psychiatric patient communicated his feelings through this drawing.

Police officers and military personnel often depend on each other for support. Those who have experienced similar pain and danger can understand and help each other.

After the fire, Rory had begun communicating his pain and frustration through artwork. He said that there were no words to describe what he sometimes felt in his missing arm, so on days when the pain was really bad, he picked up a paintbrush with his other hand and painted what he felt. He said he would become so absorbed in these paintings that eventually he would not feel the pain anymore.

Kara said that after the shooting she spent a long time in therapy trying to deal with her emotions. She felt horrible guilt for killing a person, even if he was a murderer. But she felt even guiltier that she hadn't been able to save her partner, that she had lived but he had died. She thought she deserved all the pain that she felt and even more. In therapy she began to realize she was in fact bringing at

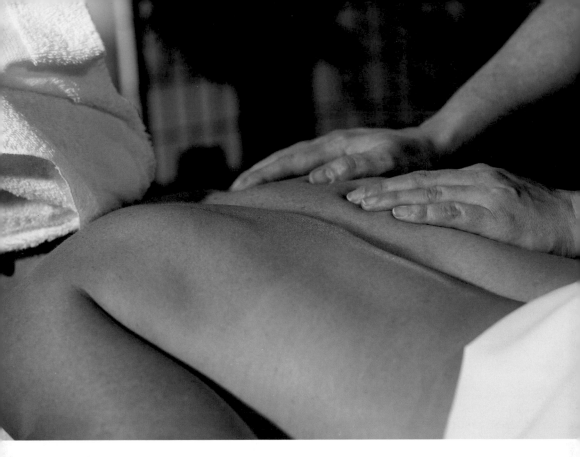

Massage therapy may help those with psychosomatic disorders better cope with their pain. Supplemental therapies like massage should not replace major therapy.

Patients should be careful when using benign treatments to identify which treatments are targeting the actual causes of their disorders and which treatments only target symptoms. It can be extremely helpful to incorporate treatments that target symptoms, such as massage for aching muscles, into part of the treatment program as long as those treatments are used as supplements to major therapy rather than substitutes for the major therapy.

Those with psychosomatic disorders may try many solutions to their pain. When drugs and painkillers do not work, they may even consider ending the pain permanently with an overdose.

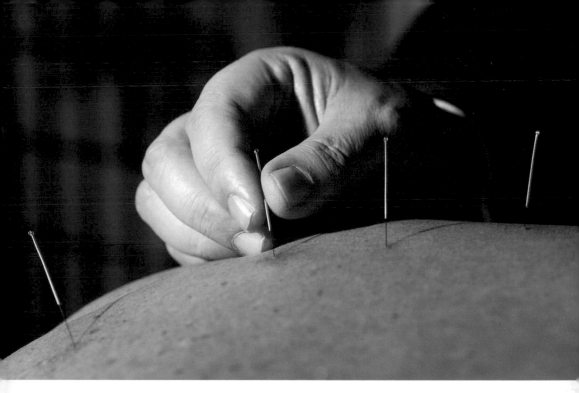

An acupuncturist inserts needles to correct the body's energy flow.

least some of this pain upon herself as a punishment for simply surviving. She said that learning to recognize that her partner's death was not her fault and that she still had the opportunity to help other people, even if she could only do it from behind a desk, was helping her to overcome her phantom-limb pain.

When Donald began to talk, everybody listened. He seemed like a legend to them—a man who had been on the D-day beaches and could still tell the story of that day and all that had happened after. He told them of all the isolation he had felt when he should have been feeling like a hero. He spoke of the physical and emotional pain that haunted him. He said that having no legs trapped his body, and the images of war trapped his mind. Over the years, he had tried every therapy, surgery, and medicine he could find. In the first years after the war, he was addicted to morphine, and then to alcohol; then he contemplated suicide. Donald said that what finally helped his pain was a combination of acupuncture and meditation. What helped his soul was developing a spiritual outlook on life. Donald spoke with belief in the power and energy of the mind. When he said that the mind was larger than the body could ever be, the whole group listened.

After their first meeting together, the four decided to meet again in one month. Then they met a month after that, and then the following month. Kevin could not tell if the pain in his leg was growing less or if he was simply learning to handle it better. What he did know was that as each month passed, his outlook on life grew more positive and his focus on the pain diminished. Since he and Donald lived in the same city, they began to meet more often. Donald suggested that Kevin come with him to the acupuncturist one day, and soon after that Donald began coaching Kevin in meditation and visualization techniques for controlling his pain. The next time their support group met, Kevin told his three new friends that meeting them truly had saved his life.

Discussion

Group therapy is now considered one of the most beneficial supplementary treatments for somatoform disorders. Many doctors believe that somatoform disorders arise from the combination of repressing mental and emotional stresses and the need to communicate with others. Group therapy provides a forum for communicating concerns about health and life in general to others. Furthermore, in group therapy all of the participants are dealing with the same type of disorder and can provide an understanding support network in which fears, goals, and treatments can be shared. Group therapy can also break the social isolation that many individuals with somatoform disorders feel. Kevin benefits so much from speaking with others like himself that he credits his new friendships with saving his life.

As already discussed, many benign treatments are also used as supplements to the major psychiatric and drug therapies. Benign

Getting together to share a meal and conversation with others who have gone through similar pain can be as healing as any drug. Research indicates that some form of formal or casual group therapy can be one of the most successful forms of supplemental treatment for those who suffer from psychosomatic disorders.

"Natural" medicines are growing in popularity across North America.

treatments include things like vitamins, nutritional supplements, cold packs for aching muscles, hot baths for relaxation, and thera-peutic massage.

As already discussed, medications are often used as a treatment both for somatoform disorders and for conditions that may coexist with these disorders. For some people, however, medication is not an option. There are a number of herbal and other natural alternatives that people use for conditions like depression and anxiety—condi-tions that could be responsible for or result from psychosomatic disorders. One of these natural alternatives is Saint-John's-wort.

Saint-John's-wort has been used for many centuries in treat-ing both physical and mental illnesses. This herb has been used in Greece, China, Europe, and North America. Studies in Europe have found Saint-John's-wort to be very effective in treating depression

Homeopathic Treatment for Psychiatric Disorders

Homeopathy is a form of alternative medicine that looks at disease and disorders from a very different perspective from conventional medicine. It treats a person's entire physical and mental being, rather than dividing a patient into various symptoms and disorders. Homeopathic medicine uses tiny doses to stimulate the body's ability to heal itself. In some cases, these doses may be administered only once every few months or years. Homeopathic practitioners believe their approach offers safe, natural alternatives that can supplement or replace conventional pharmaceutical treatment for psychiatric problems. Homeopathic medicines have few side effects, unlike the strong chemicals used for psychiatric drugs.

and anxiety, but the U.S. Food and Drug Administration has not approved it for such treatments. Although it can be purchased over the counter in health food, grocery, and drug stores, one should still do careful research before beginning any medicinal regimen.

Another herb that has been used as a natural remedy for depression and anxiety is kava. Kava is a member of the pepper family and grows in the South Pacific islands. Kava root seems to have a calming effect on the mind. It is also used as a muscle relaxant for the body. In European studies, kava root was said to have the beneficial properties of the antianxiety medication known as benzodiazepines without their negative side effects. In very high doses,

regimen: A regular course of action, systematic plan.

Chamomile and valerian are two plants used as sleep aids and to treat anxiety.

Some people turn to alternative treatments such as herbs to avoid the negative side effects of medications, but herbs can also have negative side effects. In the case of psychosomatic disorders, a patient may be just as likely to experience psychosomatic side effects from herbal remedies as from psychiatric medications.

however, kava may have side effects of its own, including sleepiness and skin irritation. Like Saint-John's-wort, it can be purchased over the counter but has not been approved for medicinal use by the Food and Drug Administration.

Valerian is yet another herb that has been used for centuries both as a sleep aid and as a temporary remedy for anxiety. It seems to act as a sedative, but as with most herbal remedies is not approved by the Food and Drug Administration for medicinal use.

There are many other herbal remedies for conditions such as depression and anxiety, but just because a remedy is said to be "natural" doesn't mean that it is safe. Many of our current medications are made from substances that were originally obtained from plants, minerals, and other natural substances. Herbs can have powerful effects on the body and can interact with other medications.

You can find more information on herbal remedies at your library or online. One should always remember, however, that there are many options a person has before resorting to drugs and complicated herbal remedies. If psychosomatic symptoms, depression, anxiety, and other difficulties plague you, look at your lifestyle first. Many people are able to obtain relief by making simple but significant changes in the way they live. Do you get a proper amount of sleep? Do you get that sleep at appropriate times (from 10 p.m. to 6 a.m. versus 3 a.m. to 1 p.m.)? Do you eat a healthy diet that is rich in fruits and vegetables and low in fats and sugars? Do you exercise regularly and spend some time outdoors every day?

Sometimes, especially in the case of psychosomatic disorders, the smallest first steps are the most important ones in changing our lives. Living a healthy lifestyle can make treating a psychosomatic disorder easier and more effective.

Further Reading

Allen, Thomas E., Mayer C. Liebman, Lee Crandall Park, and William C. Wimmer. *A Primer on Mental Disorders: A Guide for Educators, Families, and Students*. Lanham, Md.: The Scarecrow Press, 2001.

Beiling, Catherine. *A Condition of Doubt: The Meanings of Hypochondria*. New York: Oxford University Press, 2012.

Mindell, Earl, and Virginia Hopkins. *Prescription Alternatives: Hundreds of Safe, Natural, Prescription-free Remedies to Restore Your Health and Energy*. New York: McGraw-Hill, 2009.

Shapiro, Deb. *Your Body Speaks Your Mind: Decoding the Emotional, Psychological, and Spiritual Messages That Underlie Illness*. Boulder, Colo.: Sounds True, 2006.

Shorter, Edward. *From the Mind into the Body: The Cultural Origins of Psychosomatic Symptoms*. New York: Free Press, 1994.

Showalter, Elaine. *Hystories: Hysterical Epidemics and Modern Culture*. New York: Columbia University Press, 1997.

For More Information

ALLPSYCH ONLINE: The Virtual Psychology Classroom
allpsych.com/disorders/somatoform

MedScape Reference
emedicine.medscape.com/article/294908-overview

Mental-Health-Matters.com
www.mental-health-matters.com/disorders/somatoform-disorders

The Merck Manual of Diagnosis and Therapy
www.merck.com/mrkshared/mmanual/home.jsp

Psyweb.com
www.psyweb.com/Mdisord/somatd.html

Publisher's Note:
The websites listed on this page were active at the time of publication. The publisher is not responsible for websites that have changed their address or discontinued operation since the date of publication. The publisher will review and update the websites upon each reprint.

Index

About the Author & Consultants

Autumn Libal is a graduate of Smith College and the author of many educational books. She lives and works in Canada.

Mary Ann McDonnell, Ph.D., R.N., is the owner of South Shore Psychiatric Services, where she provides psychiatric services to children and adolescents. She has worked as a psychiatric nurse at Franciscan Hospital for Children and has been a clinical instructor for Northeastern University and Boston College advanced-practice nursing students. She was also the director of clinical trials in the pediatric psychopharmacology research unit at Massachusetts General Hospital. Her areas of expertise are bipolar disorder in children and adolescents, ADHD, and depression.

Donald Esherick has worked in regulatory affairs at Rhone-Poulenc Rorer, Wyeth Pharmaceuticals, Pfizer, and Pharmalink Consulting. He specializes in the chemistry section (manufacture and testing) of investigational and marketed drugs.